Praise for *The Pastor's Family*

Brian and Cara Croft provide a frank and helpful discussion of the challenges faced by pastors and their families day after day. For pastors in training, this book provides a realistic framework for future ministry. For pastors on the field, it provides encouragement and wisdom from a couple who is walking the same path as you. For church members, it provides an invaluable glimpse into the dynamics of a pastor's life. Highly recommended.

> **Timothy Paul Jones**, PhD, associate vice president and professor of leadership at The Southern Baptist Theological Seminary

I know Brian as an effective, compassionate pastor of a vital church in Louisville, and I am thrilled he and Cara have written this book to assist pastors in meeting the practical, day-to-day challenges of ministry and the often complex demands of doing life together as a ministry couple. Read it as a couple and do the exercises together. It will take your relationship and your ministry to a new level. I just wish this book had been around when I was serving as a senior minister.

> **Bob Russell**, retired senior minister at Southeast Christian Church in Louisville, Kentucky

Realistic. Honest. Transparent. Spiritual. Practical. These are the words that sprang to my mind as I read this unique book that will refresh many pastors' souls, rescue many pastors' marriages, transform many pastors' families, and revive many pastors' ministries.

> **David P. Murray**, professor of Old Testament and practical theology at Puritan Reformed Theological Seminary

All throughout the history of the church there have been pastors, so many pastors, who have sacrificed their families on the altar of ministry. Too many neglected wives and forsaken children can testify to men who time and time again chose ministry in place of family. Every pastor can testify to the power of this temptation, which is exactly why Brian and Cara Croft's book is urgently needed. *The Pastor's Family* challenges pastors to care first and best for their wives and children, and it carefully draws on biblical wisdom to allow them to do that very thing. It is a book I will read with my wife, and one I heartily recommend to every pastor.

> **Tim Challies**, pastor of Grace Fellowship Church in Toronto, Ontario, and author of *The Next Story*

the pastor's family

Shepherding Your Family through the Challenges of Pastoral Ministry

brian & cara croft

ZONDERVAN®

ZONDERVAN

The Pastor's Family

This title is also available as a Zondervan ebook.
Visit www.zondervan.com/ebooks.

This title is also available in a Zondervan audio edition.
Visit www.zondervan.fm.

Requests for information should be addressed to:

Zondervan, *Grand Rapids, Michigan 49530*

Library of Congress Cataloging-in-Publication Data

Croft, Brian.
The pastor's family : shepherding your family through the challenges of pastoral ministry / Brian and Cara Croft.
pages cm.
ISBN 978-0-310-49509-3 (pbk.)
1. Clergy—Family relationships. 2. Families of clergy. I. Title.
BV4396.C76 2013
253'.22—dc23 2013003072

Cover design: Ron Huizinga
Cover photography: Image Source/GettyImages
Interior design: Ben Fetterley and Greg Johnson/Textbook Perfect

Printed in the United States of America

14 15 16 17 /DCI/ 22 21 20 19 18 17 16 15 14 13 12 11 10 9 8 7 6 5 4 3

In loving memory of
Jackson and Barbara Boyett—

and in dedication to
the faithful saints at Auburndale Baptist Church.
Thank you for continuing to support and
encourage us as we try to care for you.

contents

foreword

Every family must adjust its lifestyle based on the parents' profession. A baker's family must adjust to the baker having to be out of the house and at work before dawn, kneading and preparing dough to rise, making pie crust and icings and fillings and biscuits for the first customers. A military family must adjust to not seeing a parent on a tour of duty for weeks and months at a time. A police officer's family must adjust to the emotional toll on their loved one from seeing crime up close and personal, day in and day out. Both police and military families must cope with a parent putting his or her life on the line to serve and protect their community and country, not knowing if they'll return home at the end of a tour or shift. A doctor's family must adjust to an unpredictable schedule, emergency calls that interrupt family time, and the constant stress that husband and dad experiences from dealing with illness or loss. An executive and his or her family must invest a lot of time and planning into maintaining a lifestyle of keeping clients and colleagues satisfied, dealing with business trips, and attending or hosting dinner parties.

Many other examples are out there — among them is the pastor's family. Yet the pastor and his family tend to face pressures that span a number of professions. Like the baker, he's up at the crack of dawn, kneading his own heart with prayer and God's Word to prepare to serve the church. Like the military man and police officer, he often places his well-being on the line to serve and protect others, often not able to give details about the pain and suffering he witnesses on a regular basis. As with the doctor, his schedule is unpredictable, and those late-night emergency calls must be answered. As with the executive, meetings and church functions lead to long hours and fatigue. The pastor's life, like that of those in many other professions, is full and busy and tiring.

Two veteran pastors capture this pressure well:

> The pastor stands alone, different from the politician, the social worker, the entrepreneur, the engineer, the physician, and the jurist. All these deal with a segment — a significant segment — of the human enterprise, but the pastor — alone — steps back from it all, examines it from God's perspective, and tries to give it all meaning, purpose, and direction. And he accomplishes this without physical power or civil authority. The pastor has only the power of example, the power of trust, the power of respect, and the power of the love of God shed abroad in Jesus Christ.[1]

Anyone who takes pastoral ministry seriously feels the spiritual responsibility and accountability the pastor bears before God for the souls of those entrusted to him. This perspective and weight make the pastor's job unique. The pastor feels the multiple expectations of his church, his own family, and the larger community, as well as his own self-imposed demands. The pastor needs a lot of help to think clearly about his life, priorities, and well-being.

This is where Brian and Cara Croft step in to help us. Pastors and their families need a book like this — a kind of field manual — that speaks to the various demands and expectations they face and provides gospel-centered, family-focused guidance. This book delves into the hearts of each member of the pastor's household and offers helpful counsel in shepherding each one according to God's Word, so that the family can serve together joyfully in the work of the ministry.

Prepare to learn as you join this transparent, insightful, conversational tour of the challenges pastors and their families face in Christian ministry. We're happy to commend not only this book but Brian and Cara as well for modeling so much of what is recommended here. They've been not only friends but also examples in this vital area of our lives — the pastor and his family.

Thabiti and Kristie Anyabwile
December 2012

a note from brian

Another book on the family?

This may have been your reaction when you first saw this book. Fair enough. I agree. The market has been flooded recently with a renewed focus on the family. A number of excellent books — and some less than excellent ones — have appeared in recent years. So why add to the madness with yet another book?

I believe the aim of this book is unique, serving a special purpose that most family books don't serve. It's a unique book because it's about a unique kind of family — the family of a *pastor*. This is a book written for men who have answered the call to serve the church of God as preachers, teachers, leaders, and shepherds. And it's written to address a unique problem these church leaders face: How do you faithfully serve the church while serving your family? How do you balance the demands of ministry with the demands of being a father and husband? How do you prioritize your time between preaching the Word, making disciples, and loving your wife and children?

Pastoral ministry is more challenging than ever today, with burdens and expectations that many pastors didn't experience in previous generations. Many aspiring pastors start out in ministry with great zeal for the work God has called them to do, but the difficult demands and pressures of ministry overwhelm them and they quickly crash and burn, leaving them with a battered faith and a broken family. This book is written to call the pastor to the priority of shepherding his family while still faithfully serving the church. Our belief is that it is possible to do both. We have tried to identify the unique challenges of pastoral ministry, diagnosing the causes that lead to tension between the family and the church, and we propose biblical solutions. Before we jump into all this, however, let me give you some context for the advice shared in the pages that follow.

First, be warned that I am *not* an expert on this subject. I am a husband, yes. And I am a father and a pastor. I regularly fail at each of these roles. If you have picked up this book in the hope that I will have all of the solutions to the struggles in your life and ministry, you will be disappointed. I write this, not as an expert, but simply as a husband, father, and pastor who has a deep desire to faithfully learn by God's grace in each of these areas. The suggestions I offer are merely that — suggestions to serve as a template for you to apply in your own specific family and ministry context. Perhaps God will use my failures and the lessons I have learned to bless others. I am trusting they will be received by those who read this with the awareness that I am a sinner saved by God's grace, one who is still in the trenches fighting for joy and faithfulness in family and ministry.

Second, this work is not intended to create an "us versus them" mentality between the pastor's family and the local church. Though this is the tension many pastors feel — the pull between the responsibilities of family and the demands of the church — I do not believe this is a necessary tension. My family and I had some difficult years when we first arrived at the church where I now serve. We were entering a struggling, declining church, and I proceeded to make many "rookie" mistakes. Those early years were a time of struggle but also a time of learning many of the painful lessons I write about in this book. I share these experiences, not to reinforce a negative perception of the local church, but to show that it is necessary to struggle through this tension and arrive at a healthy balance. I believe pastors should love their churches and the people they serve, regardless of the challenges of ministry. Our family deeply loves our church, where we have now served for over a decade. But we love it even more today because we grew and matured through the struggles we share in this book.

Third, the content of this book is not intended to encourage anyone to pursue an "easy" ministry post. As local churches train up men for ministry, they should not just identify those who are called; they must train and prepare them to go into the hard places where others will not go. We want to raise up pastors who will plant themselves and persist in dysfunctional local churches. We aim to prepare missionaries who will sacrifice and take the gospel to the unreached places where persecution is almost certain. Although this book calls ministers of the gospel to prioritize and sacrifice for the sake of their family, it should not be taken as an endorsement of the notion that we can avoid the hardship of sacrifice in ministry. Ministry *is* hard. Sacrifice is *always* necessary. This book is meant to equip pastors to shepherd their family through the difficulties and sufferings they will encounter in ministry, not try to avoid them.

If you are called and gifted for ministry, you must not avoid the pursuit of your call in the name of saving your family from the challenges of ministry. I once heard about a young man who was very gifted for pastoral ministry. He deeply loved his family and was being offered several ministry opportunities. After sifting through these opportunities, he refused them all, citing the same concern in each case: "I cannot take my family there." He simply ended up not going anywhere. My desire is that this book will awaken the hearts of pastors, missionaries, and Christian men to the glorious responsibility of shepherding their family. At the same time, I've tried to balance this responsibility against the sinful tendency to idolize the family, something that is just as sinful, harmful, and dishonoring to God as neglect.

Now a final word about my writing companion. One of the best ways to read this book is together as husband and wife. Throughout the book, my wife has shared her invaluable insights and perspectives on the joys, struggles, and realities of being a mother and wife in a pastor's family. I hope you learn from her wisdom and thoughtfulness, both of which I am blessed to receive daily! I trust that both pastors and their wives will be able to interact with this book, as we have throughout the writing process. In other words, expect gracious interruptions and insightful additions about family and ministry life.

I hope you enjoy the friendly and spirited exchanges and can relate to both our successes and failures. Most of all, I hope you come to see that true success, enjoyment, faithfulness, and longevity in any pastor's ministry begin and end at the same place — with your life together as a family.

Brian Croft
Louisville, Kentucky
August 2012

a note from cara

Recently, a new couple who had moved to town so the husband could attend seminary visited our church. As his wife and I were chatting about their move, their family, and the life of ministry, she asked me a question: "Is ministry easier or more difficult than you expected?" It was a great question. And a challenging one to answer. I thought about it for a moment and responded truthfully, "It is more rewarding than I expected."

The truth is that life in ministry has been both harder and easier than we anticipated it would be. The life of ministry is a hard life. There is no question about that. The pressures faced by a pastor's family are different from the pressures faced by those in other occupations. But unique joys also come with this calling. I once heard someone describe the joys of pastoral ministry by saying that we get a front-row seat to what God is doing, and I've found this to be true. It's difficult walking through marital problems with a couple, seeing the brokenness and pain in their lives and the effect it has on their children. And yet we are able to rejoice with them as God heals their marriage and restores their love and trust for one another. We weep with the woman who suffers a miscarriage, and then with joy we celebrate as, years later, she holds her firstborn. Walking with people through struggle and loss is hard, but it provides countless opportunities for us to experience firsthand the joy of seeing God's answers to prayers.

Would I have chosen this path for my family? My honest answer is no. I would never have chosen to be in this position. As a matter of fact, when my husband first told me about his desire to be a pastor, I fought it! There was no way I was ever going to be a pastor's wife. However, I am thankful that God knows what I need better than I do. I would have missed out on much had God left me to my own wisdom — to simply do what I wanted. The truth is that I am very thankful for our life as the family of a pastor. I am very thankful for my husband and for our church. My children love our church. No other body of Christians is as dear to my heart as the people of our church. And there is no other place we would rather be, no other group of people we would rather serve. Experiencing this deep sense of love for this ministry and for our church has been a process, a work that God has done in my life over time.

I became involved in the writing of this book for several reasons. First of all, my husband asked me to, and I find it difficult to say no to him. Second, I've learned many things as a woman, wife, and mother that offer a different perspective from his as a man, husband, and father. We are different, but our experiences and insights complement one another as we write from common convictions about the gospel and what the Scriptures teach. We've taken this journey on the road of ministry together, so it seemed fitting that we write this book together as well.

In addition to reading an entire chapter on the struggles and joys of being a pastor's wife (chapter 3), you will find my various "interruptions" scattered throughout the pages of this book. These are intended to be gracious interruptions, offered with respect and love, to complement what Brian is saying by offering my own perspective. Do I do this when we talk in real life? Yes. Since we are communicating through writing and not talking directly with you, it can be hard to read my tone, but let me assure you that I greatly respect and admire my husband as the leader of our home — and as my own pastor!

You may be wondering who I am. Brian and I have been married for over sixteen years. I am a homeschooling mother to four wonderful children — one son and three daughters (you can start praying for my son now!). I am the daughter (and daughter-in-law) of very committed, God-fearing Christian parents. I am a chauffeur who spends hours each day shuttling children to their various sports and activities. I am an amateur photographer, when I have the time. I am a friend who is sometimes fiery and opinionated, but I always want to share my thoughts in a respectful way. I am a listener, a shoulder for someone to cry on. And, yes, I am also a pastor's wife. Not the bread-making, choir-singing, piano-playing type of pastor's wife you may have envisioned, but nonetheless the wife of my husband, Brian, who pastors our church.

As shocking as it may be, I have plenty of faults as well. Just ask my kids! I am sure they will be glad to fill you in on all of them. I accept that I am a flawed, imperfect, and sinful woman, but I know all of this is covered by the sanctifying blood of Jesus. I rely daily on God's grace for wisdom, strength, and courage to face whatever may come our way. Though I wish I did, I do not have all the answers. I give flawed advice, though sometimes it is good and helpful to people. It's important to realize that every ministry situation is unique, just as every marriage and every family are! Some of the principles we share will apply across the board to all readers, but many of the specifics regarding how the application plays out will differ from person to person. Don't try to make your marriage and your ministry like ours. Rather, our hope is that you can learn from our mistakes and failures and from the wisdom we share, applying it to your own unique context.

As my husband said in his note, ministry is hard. Sacrifice is always necessary. And I would add one final thought to that: The rewards are eternal! I pray that this book will encourage you, spurring you on to greater love for your family and your church. I pray that it will cause you and your spouse to have meaningful, intentional conversations about your marriage and your family. I pray that it will cause you to persevere in this race we are running as we strive to finish and win. And above all, I pray that it will glorify God and cause you to rely even more on his limitless and amazing grace.

Cara Croft
Louisville, Kentucky
August 2012

introduction

what is *faithful* ministry?

{brian}

One of the most meaningful forms of encouragement for my Christian walk is reading Christian biographies. We find examples of grace and divine strength in the stories of heroic men and women who sacrificed much to embody Jesus' call to deny themselves and take up their cross and follow him (Mark 8:34). We seek to emulate those who throughout the centuries served in hostile churches for the sake of caring for souls, traveled thousands of miles through dangerous terrain to preach the gospel to those who had never heard it, labored tirelessly to translate God's Word into the common language amid constant threats on their lives, and who even gave their very lives for the sake of Christ.

No doubt, the bar for greatness in the kingdom of God in our eyes is set by these giants of our faith. The lives of pastors like Jonathan Edwards, John Bunyan, Charles Spurgeon, and Richard Baxter; evangelists like George Whitefield and John Wesley; missionaries like William Carey, John Paton, and Adoniram Judson; Reformers like John Calvin and Martin Luther; and theologians like Augustine, John Owen, and B. B. Warfield all increase our desire to do something great for the sake of Christ, as well as to be found faithful in the end by our Redeemer. Yet, what does it mean to be faithful to the end? What does true greatness look like in the eyes of our Savior and King?

Whether we evaluate someone's ministry from the past or in the present, we tend to rate the greatness of the evangelist based on how many people were converted under his ministry. We crown theologians as those with the greatest impact on history and the church based on the insightfulness of their writings and how much they published. We celebrate missionaries and highlight their accounts of sufferings, conversions, and churches planted. We idolize pastors who preached to the masses or wrote books that were notable or memorable. In other words, we end up defining greatness much like the world does — by how grand, glamorous, and broad an impact an individual had in their life and ministry.

Yet the Bible's definitions of greatness and faithfulness seem much different. The classic example of this paradox of worldly and godly greatness can be seen in Jesus' response to his disciples as they argued about who among them would be greatest in the kingdom of God (Mark 9:33 – 37; 10:35 – 40). Jesus shattered their understanding of greatness by saying, "Whoever wants to become great among you must be your servant" (Mark 10:43). Think about it. What does a servant do? There is nothing glamorous about being a servant. Rarely will we find world-changing influence and broad-sweeping impact in the work of a servant. In fact, servants do much of what we call "grunt work." Servants do the jobs no one else wants to do. And they often do them when no one else is looking.

This, along with several similar biblical texts, raises a question: What if God evaluates the success or failure of a ministry differently than we do? What if God were to measure an evangelist's faithfulness, not based on the amount of conversions he saw in his ministry, but on his daily commitment to walk with God? What if God determined the greatness of a missionary, not based on the global effects of his ministry, but on his relentless pursuit of godliness and his battle against sin and the Enemy? What if God evaluated the faithfulness and greatness of a pastor, not simply by the successes of his local church ministry, but by how well he cared for and pastored his own family—his wife and his children?

For many pastors and church leaders, the care of the family seems to fall under that category of plain, servantlike grunt work that goes largely unnoticed when we assess the greatness of our heroes of the past. If you doubt this is true, try comparing how much you know about the family lives of these celebrated men to the content of their teaching or the impact of their ministries. As I began doing research for this book, I talked with some well-known church historians, and they all told me the same thing when I asked about several of the notable leaders of the past: "There just isn't much out there about their families." So I think it's safe to assume that our process for determining if someone is "great and faithful" in ministry is typically not dependent on whether these men were faithful to love their wives and shepherd their children.

The classic example is found in the contrast between the ministry of the eighteenth-century evangelist and pastor John Wesley and his marriage. Wesley is celebrated for how God used him to bring about the conversion of many people throughout the United Kingdom and America. He started the far-reaching Methodist movement that is still active today. Yet Wesley was not shy when articulating his view of marriage. He wrote these words in a journal entry on March 19, 1751: "I cannot understand how a Methodist preacher can answer it [sic] to God to preach one sermon or travel one day less in a married than in a single state. In this respect surely 'it remaineth that they who have wives be as though they had none.'"[2]

Wesley wrote this comment just one month into his marriage, and unfortunately, his "disdain" for marriage did not seem to wane over the years that followed. Years later, Wesley wrote to a young preacher about to be married to discourage the efforts of his future bride who might seek to prevent him from traveling to preach.[3] Wesley's marriage philosophy proved to have the expected ramifications. His relationship with his own wife was a mess for most of their lives, which led to her efforts to sabotage his reputation and ministry on numerous occasions. Based on what little we know of Wesley's wife, Molly, she does not appear to be the most spiritually sound, warm, and gracious of individuals. Nevertheless, John Wesley's treatment of her throughout their marriage, and what appears to be his complete disregard of the biblical mandates to care for his wife, should have ruined him, his reputation, and his legacy. Yet for most Methodist churchgoers today, Wesley's horrific marriage is commonly overlooked.[4]

Lest we assume Wesley's views were simply a product of his theology, we should note that one of his contemporaries also struggled with marriage. Although John Wesley and George Whitefield contended with one another over the doctrines of Calvinism, they shared common ground in their view of marriage and its purpose in their lives and ministries. George Whitefield delayed marriage for many years because he did not want marriage to hinder his highly demanding preaching ministry throughout the world. When he finally entered into marriage, it was with the understanding that his marriage to Elizabeth James would "not be allowed to hinder his ministry in the least."[5] Of course, any married man knows this sentiment is not a realistic expectation on which to build a solid foundation for love and respect, and this faulty supposition led to further disappointment and reinforced his view that marriage was a bothersome hindrance to ministry. Arnold Dallimore, Whitefield's biographer, wrote:

> Whitefield manifestly found his determination not to let marriage affect his ministry in the slightest way, impossible to carry out. Try as he might, he could not avoid occasions when being married demanded some revision of his plans and prevented the fulfillment of some intended schedule of preaching. And finding it necessary even once or twice to say, "I have married a wife, and therefore I cannot come," he became disappointed and though he looked on marriage as largely a help, he also considered it a hindrance."[6]

Whitefield's marriage views did not wreak the same degree of havoc in his life as Wesley's did in his; yet, the result was still a very unhappy, disappointed wife — one who in large part did not feel cared for by her husband.[7]

Missionaries have also struggled with the challenges of ministry and marriage, often giving a theological rationale for their decision to prioritize evangelism and ministry over the care of their families. The man given the distinguished title of "the Father of Modern Missions," William Carey, almost abandoned his pregnant wife,

Dorothy, and his children to pursue his missionary work in India. Carey's wife did eventually concede to go, but his lack of care for her and the rigors of missionary life drove her to experience depression, psychological issues, and eventual insanity. Biographer Doreen Moore gives the details:

> It started with a five-month sea voyage where she was seasick most of the time. When they arrived in Calcutta, their inadequate funds were quickly depleted, forcing his family to live in a rundown place outside of Calcutta. Even worse, the other missionaries lived in relative affluence in Calcutta. His wife complained because they had to "live without many of… the necessaries of life, bread in particular." Dorothy was also afflicted with dysentery and their oldest son almost died from it. Later, Carey moved his wife, infant, and three sons under ten, into an untamed malarial-infested region where alligators, tigers, and huge poisonous snakes were in abundance. They moved soon after to Mudnabatti where Dorothy again became ill. But far worse, their five-year-old son Peter died. After this devastating loss, Dorothy Carey's mental health declined. She never recovered but deteriorated to such an extent that she was described as "wholly deranged." William Carey believed "the cause of Christ" took precedence over his family.[8]

Our point in sharing these examples from the past is not to criticize the particular decisions and choices these men made. It is simply to point out that the temptation to prioritize ministry over family is not new. These are men whom we celebrate as great and faithful laborers for the sake of Christ, but whose marriages and families were sacrificed — for noble reasons — on the altar of their ministry. Their apparent failures as husbands and fathers should not lead us to discount all that the Lord did through these men. God uses sinful, imperfect men and women to bring about his sovereign purposes for his glory, and he has done this throughout history and continues to do it today. Still, these examples point to the fact that the temptation to elevate ministry concerns above family commitments is a persistent problem, one that is easily ignored in our current church culture. We tend to ignore the failed examples of these men with regard to their responsibilities as husbands and fathers simply because they did "great things" for God. And it is all too easy to make the same mistake in our own churches and in our own families.

My point is not to dredge up mistakes of the past. It's to suggest that the temptations a pastor or church leader faces to neglect his family for the sake of greater and more fruitful ministry are nothing new. Any pastor, missionary, or evangelist who burns with passion to do great things for God will sense this tension. It's symptomatic of the cultural disconnect between our public success in ministry and our more private family life. And unfortunately, this disconnect is rooted in something even more powerful than our contemporary church culture. We need to take a closer look at the relationship between a pastor's ministry and his family by getting to the root of why church leaders are tempted to sacrifice their wives and children on the altar of ministry. The problem must be diagnosed before we can determine the solution. That's what we'll cover in chapter 1. Once the true root of the problem is identified, we'll seek in chapter 2 a biblical solution, one that relies on the power of the gospel and on Scripture's clear mandates for Christian husbands and fathers, especially those who are pastors.

For the remainder of the book we will look at the specific and unique challenges that every pastor, his wife, and their children are certain to experience. We'll talk about several clear, practical strategies for a man to shepherd his family through these challenges (chapters 3 – 6). Our hope is that these suggestions will help you avoid the regrets that inevitably come when you neglect your family during the difficult seasons of ministry (chapter 7). And lest you assume I have carelessly criticized some of the most celebrated heroes of the church, I will be lifting up several other men from the past who had an equally monumental impact on the world for the sake of Christ, yet who have done so with an inspiring faithfulness to love their wives and shepherd their children.

Before we get to practical strategies for faithful ministry, we must first tackle the problem. Why do so many pastors struggle to balance the call to shepherd faithfully the church with the call to care responsibly and lovingly for their wives and children? Why is this so hard? We'll consider these questions in the next chapter as we take a closer look at the heart of a pastor. What lies within the hearts of those called to shepherd God's people?

part 1

the pastor's heart

"It's Not You—It's Me"

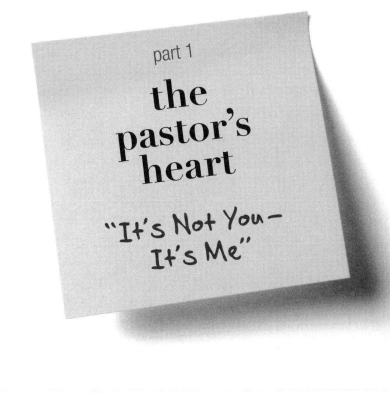

chapter 1

the problem

{brian}

Early in my ministry as a pastor, I found that the most noticeable problems typically get the most attention. In other words, "the squeaky wheel gets the grease." Though this maxim originally referred to the regular maintenance of a tractor or car, it is certainly true when it comes to pastoral ministry in a local church. The day-to-day reality of pastoral ministry generally means a pastor must tend to the immediate and pressing needs of his congregation. For most pastors, their schedule is determined by focusing on the most obvious problems. Those that seem the most problematic are the ones that get his attention.

I won't try to deny any of this. Let's be honest as we begin — a pastor should prioritize the most immediate needs in his church. I'll admit this is how I often determine what I'm going to do on any given day. If I have to choose between a weekly discipleship meeting with a young man in the church who is battling loneliness and a visit with an elderly lady who is dying from cancer, I'll go to the hospital every time. Even though the choices may not always be this obvious, scenarios like this one tend to define much of the pressure a pastor feels each and every day. A pastor knows he needs to meet with that young man — he needs to be making long-term investments that will bear fruit over time — but he also knows there is a dying woman who needs him. The demands on those who pastor are always greater than what they can meet. This tends to create some default patterns in which "the squeaky wheels" of ministry get the grease, so to speak, while other, equally important areas of responsibility are less attended.

Often, the pastor's family is the wheel that squeaks the least. Why is this so? Most pastors' wives are keenly aware of the demands of ministry. More so than any other member of the church, a pastor's wife is aware of how hard her husband labors to care for the flock. And because she wants to support and encourage her husband, she is gracious, not wanting to add to the pressures that already exist. In the midst of these demands, pressures, and expectations, a pastor's family can easily get squeezed out. A pastor may not even be aware that it's happening, at least not at first.

There are many demands on a pastor's time, and most of them are legitimate. Yet the real problem of neglect is actually rooted in something deeper than just competing demands for time and attention. The problem is something that is innate to our nature, something that does not vanish with better planning and more deliberate delegation of pastoral responsibilities. Getting organized won't fix this. Learning to manage your time won't solve it.

Before we address the root of the problem, we'll look at the demands that commonly pull on a pastor's conscience. What are the competing demands faced by pastors? What makes them so compelling? So tempting?

The Demands of Approval

Everyone wants to be liked. Pastors are no different in this regard, especially when it comes to the people they have been entrusted to care for, pray for, and minister to — the people for whom they must ultimately give an account (Hebrews 13:17). But what happens when a pastor finds that those he seeks approval from (the people he shepherds) do not give it to him? He tends to follow his innate desire to be liked and accepted. I remember how this worked when I was in middle school. I had a group of friends, and I desperately wanted to be accepted by them, so I endeavored to earn their favor. I started to do things I knew would win their approval, following their suggestions and doing the things they wanted me to do. In doing so, I was regularly tempted to compromise my own convictions. Most of the time, I was more interested in being liked than in doing what was right.

Sadly, my pathetic pursuit of acceptance in middle school wasn't much different from the pull of acceptance a pastor feels toward his flock, the group of people he labors to serve. For many pastors, their entire livelihood — their financial income and position in the community — lies under the control of their congregants. Even if this isn't the case, the life of a pastor is often consumed with meeting the needs of the people he serves. Many of the sacrifices a pastor makes are for them. I am aware of this demand on my own life and regularly find myself pressured to do something I do not necessarily want to do, something that someone in the church wants me to do. A pastor who underestimates the powerful pull of the approval of his flock will also be blind to how easily this demand for approval can lead to an unhelpful and unfulfilled obsession.

{cara}

I was a bit different from Brian when I was in middle school. While I, too, felt the pressure of trying to fit in, instead of trying to change myself to fit in, I rebelled against this pressure instead of accommodating it. I refused to change and tended to withdraw from those who pressured me to change. I still wanted the approval of my friends, but I wanted them to accept me as I was. This response is just as sinful because it leads to an unhealthy focus on ourselves. We turn inward and nurse resentment or bitterness instead of reaching out to others. This response reflects a selfish heart — we "look out for number one," as the saying goes. Sometimes we become so concerned about what others might say or think of us that we become paralyzed with fear. Rather than risk changing, we do nothing. Wanting approval from others is still at the heart of the issue — even if we don't respond by changing who we are to please others.

The Demands of Appearance

It has been said that "perception is reality." Whether we like it or not, perception drives much of what a pastor does. It can have a positive effect, for an awareness that others are looking to us and our example can lead to a concern for personal holiness and help us avoid scenarios that might compromise our integrity. Taking seriously the truth that perception matters, that others are watching our lives, can encourage a pastor to give due diligence to the call to manage his household well (1 Timothy 3:4). Yet there is also a danger in caring too much for appearances, especially if it leads to an environment that stifles honest confession of sin and the need for accountability and help. Because the family of a pastor is under such close scrutiny from the church, it can be tempting for a pastor to care more about the way his family appears to other people than about actually caring for his family. Certainly, the way a pastor manages his family is important — indeed, it is a biblical qualification that confirms his calling (1 Timothy 3:2, 4 – 5). But an unhealthy focus on perception — caring *too much* for what others think — tempts a pastor to seek a quick fix or to cover up unhealthy patterns and problems instead of honestly dealing with the sins he commits and the challenges he faces in his family life.

For example, when marriage problems come to the surface, a pastor and his wife may try to put on a happy face and pretend things are fine instead of transparently dealing with their struggle. At a recent conference, a poll of more than one thousand pastors revealed that 77 percent of those surveyed felt they did not have a good marriage.[1] Knowing how difficult it is for most pastors to share their struggles with the people in their congregation, I think we can safely assume that very few of these pastors have revealed their marriage struggles to their church. To appear competent and spiritually mature, a pastor may be tempted to downplay very real problems, even to the point of ignoring sinful patterns in his life.

A pastor once shared with me about some of his church members who were becoming increasingly hostile toward him. They were trying to build a case to have him removed from the church. Some had begun driving by the church at various times to keep a record of when his car was at the church and when it wasn't, thinking they could indict him for being lazy or catch him not working. As silly as that may seem, it had a very real effect on this man. He confessed to me that he was still tempted to accommodate his critics, to prove to them that he was a hard worker. He sought to change his schedule, doing less visiting with people outside the church so he could appear to be around more. He felt compelled to do this, even if it meant compromising what he felt God was calling him to do. Perception is reality for many pastors, and it can exert great power and control over their lives, even leading to the neglect of those whom they should be shepherding.

{cara}

Wives, don't you feel this as well? Let me ask you a couple of questions. How do you feel on Sunday morning when your children are sitting with you and they seem to have ants in their pants and are talking loudly enough to be heard down the hallway? Doesn't it make you want to crawl under the pew and hide or, better yet, leave the building altogether? Do you worry about what food to bring to the potluck? Heaven forbid we overcook it! What about your house? Do you worry about what your house looks like when church members come over? There are doors my husband is forbidden to open when we have people over. If you relate to any of these scenarios, then you feel the powerful demand of "appearance" too. We want people to think we have it all together — the perfect house, the perfect kids, the perfect dog, the perfect cook. We worry about what people might say if we are anything less than perfect. This demand of appearance goes hand in hand with the demand of approval.

The Demands of Success

The demand for a pastor to be seen as "successful" may be greater in America than anywhere else in the world. In addition to our own inner need to prove we are successful, the consumeristic measuring stick of the American church that judges pastoral performance by numbers and nickels is an unhelpful and unbiblical yardstick that has little to do with kingdom fruitfulness. Sadly, the pursuit of "success" in the pastorate inevitably leads to the neglect of other priorities. And one of the priorities most commonly sacrificed in the pursuit of pastoral success is a pastor's family.

A man's identity is often equated with his level of success within his chosen occupation. A man who is unemployed or failing at his job is usually a very discouraged man. And pastors are certainly not immune to this aspect of masculine identity. Paul David Tripp, a well-known author and a pastor to pastors, explains how his early years of pastoral ministry led him to an identity crisis:

> Ministry had become my identity. No, I didn't think of myself as a child of God, in daily need of grace, in the middle of my own sanctification, still in a battle with sin, still in need of the body of Christ, and called to pastoral ministry. No, I thought of myself as a *pastor.* That's it, bottom line. The office of pastor was more than a calling and a set of God-given gifts that had been recognized by the body of Christ. "Pastor" defined me. It *was* me in a way that proved to be more dangerous than I would have thought.[2]

The crisis of identity caused by the drive to be successful is one of the main reasons many pastors feel discouraged today. Many of these men work hard and make great sacrifices, but they feel like they have little to show for it at the end of the day. In desperation, many pastors succumb to "doing whatever works" to find the success they long for in their church. Pastors who feel like a failure easily succumb to the pull of pragmatism.[3] Not only does this desperation for success breed a pragmatic mentality in ministry; it can also lead a pastor who finds that his family life isn't "working" well for him to neglect them, prioritizing the schedules, decisions, and needs of the church over those of his own wife and children.

The Demands of Significance

One of the easiest ways to discourage a pastor is to make him feel like he is unneeded. Pastors often struggle with a desire to be significant in some way. The most obvious way this surfaces is in the tendency to volunteer to do all the work. This creates an unhealthy pattern of ministry in which the pastor's need to be needed leads the church to depend on him for everything. He has to make every visit. He has to preach every Sunday. He has to be at every meeting. He has to conduct every wedding and funeral. Because of this, he will not delegate any of his tasks to others. He will not take his vacation time — even though he badly needs some time away with his family. He will not allow others to help him — even though he is close to burning out as he tries to balance the demands of church and family. His desire to be needed leads him to unconsciously create a church culture in which he seems to be irreplaceable. This can easily be camouflaged as faithfulness to the Lord or as a zeal to labor hard in the work of the ministry, yet it eventually leads to two common results: burnout and family neglect.

A pastor's need for significance can also lead to the neglect of his family when certain people in the church make him feel more significant than his wife and children do. A pastor can easily fall into this deception. He can become convinced that he really needs to meet with a young man in the church to help him work through his problems — even if it means missing dinner with the family for the third straight evening. The young man who thinks you hung the moon and hangs on every word you say can be powerfully persuasive when compared to the demands of your tired, spent wife and the cranky toddlers who await your homecoming.

The Demands of Expectation

In every local church we find two sets of expectations: the ones the church has for their pastor and the ones the pastor places on himself. These two sets of expectations are present in every church, and rarely do they match up. A pastor friend in the first year of his pastorate was once approached by two separate deacons at two separate times. One of the men came to criticize him, telling him he was not in the office enough and needed to spend more time in the building so he could be available to people stopping by the church. The other man came in to complain that he wasn't visiting the elderly members often enough and that he needed to get out more frequently to see people in their homes. Wisely, this pastor met with both of these men to discuss these conflicting demands and to talk about setting some realistic expectations instead of trying to figure out how to be in two places at the same time. That conversation proved fruitful and led to increasingly realistic expectations for the future.

As unrealistic as the expectations of a church may seem, most faithful pastors know that the most difficult expectations a pastor faces are the ones he places on himself. A pastor wants to be Superman. He thinks his people demand this of him. Personally, I know that when I'm faced with competing expectations from the people in my church, I am the one who is most disappointed at my inability to be there for everyone who needs me. Pastors commonly place unachievable, unhelpful expectations on themselves, and when you combine the expectations of the congregation with a pastor's own unrealistic, Superman mentality, it's a toxic combination — one that often leads to the neglect of the pastor's family.

{cara}

Wives, we deal with the demands of expectations too, but this plays out a bit differently for us. I think it most commonly shows up in two ways. First, a pastor's wife feels a strong pull to be overinvolved in the life of the church. Though the pastoral committee may say they're hiring only your husband, not you, it doesn't mean you don't have expectations placed on you as his wife. If there is anybody the church will want to see more than their pastor, it is his wife. After all, shouldn't she be able to head up the hospitality committee, the women's ministry, and the children's ministry — and be at every service every week? As a pastor's wife, you will need to protect your time — and your family. You cannot sacrifice your family and neglect your husband because you are so worn down from serving the church.

The second way in which these expectations show up is in our own expectations of our husbands. Are your expectations realistic? Or do you reinforce the superhero mentality, expecting your husband to be Superman? To be clear, we must be honest in communicating our needs and being open about the needs of the family, but we need to remember that our husbands cannot meet all of our needs. Be realistic about your communication (don't expect him to read your mind), and be willing to give him grace. Allow for the fact that the church will interrupt your life from time to time.

The Demands of Friendship

The only person lonelier than a pastor in a church may be the pastor's wife. While this isn't true of every pastor, it's still a common reality in ministry today. This truth is difficult for many people who are not pastors to accept. After all, their pastor is so loved by the people. Shouldn't he have the most friends in the church? And the pastor's wife is the person all the women go to for counsel. Surely she has lots of friends! Research from Focus on the Family, however, reveals that 70 percent of pastors do not have close personal friends and have no one to confide in.[4] My own experience leads me to believe that the percentage of lonely pastors' wives is even higher. But why is this true?

Being a pastor and the wife of a pastor can indeed be a very lonely position. In some circumstances, the culture of the church makes it difficult for them to have meaningful relationships where it is safe to be genuine, transparent, open with their struggles, and honest about church issues. At some large churches, serving with other pastors and their wives can create a place for this type of sharing, but in many cases the most meaningful relationships pastors and their wives will have are the ones outside of their local church.

As a result, pastors and their wives must put in extra effort to cultivate meaningful, safe friendships, both inside and outside the church. Because these friendships take extra work to develop, many pastors and their wives end up lonely, with few friends who really know what they are struggling with.

{cara}

Brian isn't saying we can't have meaningful friendships in the church. Some of our closest friends have come from the congregation we serve. However, we still need to be cautious and wise about what we share and with whom we share it.

There is an additional, unique emotion that a pastor's wife may face in this regard — envy. Some nights Brian comes home from the church exhausted. We sit down for a family dinner, and I am looking forward to some downtime with him — and then that dreaded phone rings. Sure enough, it is a church member who has suddenly been admitted to the hospital or someone whose marriage is in crisis. I watch my weary husband drag himself back out for the evening, and I sit alone, with the children, not sure when he will return home.

At these moments, it is hard not to be envious of the time these people are getting with my husband. We easily let envy into our hearts. We quickly become resentful of the time our husbands need to give. We feel like all we get is the leftovers, and sometimes even those are taken. It is easy for the wife of a pastor to grow bitter toward the church in these moments. This battle is very real and our struggle is understandable. This is why it is important that we make the extra effort to develop healthy friendships where we can be honest about these things, relationships where we can share our hurts and disappointments before they have a chance to become established and turn into bitter roots of resentment.

The demands and expectations placed on a pastor and his wife are very real, and they make it difficult to develop close relationships. But having close friends is still possible, even if it takes extra work. Pastors need to exercise wisdom, cautiously seeking out people (and couples) both within the congregation and outside it with whom they can be real and honest.

The Pastor's Real Problem

All of the demands we have considered exert a powerful pull on the hearts and minds of a pastor and his wife. The temptation to follow these demands can deceive us into making decisions that will negatively affect our families. But these demands, although powerful and consuming, are not the real enemy. In many cases, they are legitimate desires for good things — a need for love, friendship, and significance. These desires are not really the problem. The problem stems not from the demands a pastor faces but from the way he and his wife choose to respond to those demands.

In the heart of every pastor is an innate wiring, a tendency to fulfill his desires and meet the demands of life in broken, selfish, and sinful ways. This is the fundamental problem that leads a pastor to neglect his marriage and his children. It's a problem that dates back to the first marriage and the first family — to Adam and Eve. After God created the heavens, the earth, and all the living creatures (Genesis 1 – 2), he also created man and woman in his image (Genesis 1:27). This man and his wife were united together as one flesh, naked and not ashamed (Genesis 2:24 – 25). God declared all that he had made to be "very good" (Genesis 1:31), yet Adam and Eve deliberately sinned against their Creator and Lord by disobeying

God's command, eating from the tree of the knowledge of good and evil (Genesis 3:6). God had warned Adam and Eve not to eat from this tree or they would die (Genesis 2:17). But when Satan tempted Eve, she ignored God's warning and ate from the tree, giving some of its fruit to her husband (Genesis 3:6). Instead of obeying God's command, the man and his wife rebelled against God. They decided they wanted to rule their own lives, make their own decisions, and meet their own needs rather than be ruled by God and trust him.

When Adam and Eve sinned against God, sin entered the world and changed everything. All of us who have been born as children of Adam and Eve inherit their sinful hearts, living under the curse of death and decay. We are born into a fallen, sinful world with defiled hearts and a natural disposition to rebel against God and pursue the pleasures of sin. Jesus affirmed this truth about the human condition. Mark 7:1–23 describes Jesus' confrontation with the Pharisees, who were arrogantly putting their faith in their deeds and traditions. They were blinded to what Jesus said really matters to God—not the external, physical things we do, but the internal, spiritual matters of the heart.

In this context, Jesus spoke, not just about the corrupt state of our hearts, but about how this corruption affects our relationship with God. Jesus said that what goes into a person from the outside does not defile them because it doesn't go into their heart; it goes into their stomach (Mark 7:18–19). Jesus then added these words:

> "What comes out of a person is what defiles them. For it is from within, out of a person's heart, that evil thoughts come—sexual immorality, theft, murder, adultery, greed, malice, deceit, lewdness, envy, slander, arrogance and folly. All these evils come from inside and defile a person."
>
> *Mark 7:20–23*

For most of their lives, Jesus' disciples had followed strict laws and traditions that reinforced the notion that defilement came from foods and other objects that had been declared unclean. Yet Jesus taught a counterintuitive truth: that acceptance in the kingdom of God is based not on the external, but on the internal — on the state of one's heart.[5]

A pastor's heart is no different from any other heart. A pastor's neglect of his family cannot simply be blamed on the pressures, demands, and unrealistic expectations that have been placed on him. In the end, the struggle he faces — and the neglect of the family — has one root cause: a sinful heart. The reason a pastor disobeys the direct commands of Scripture to care for his family and excuses his disobedience is his sinful desire. Rather than trusting God in obedience, believing that God will meet his needs, he tries to meet his own needs for acceptance, significance, approval, and friendship. This is a pattern deeply rooted in his heart.

But what does this look like, practically speaking? Let me give some examples of specific sins a pastor might commit, sins that are closely linked to the demands of ministry we examined earlier:

- Being enslaved to the demands of approval and appearance could reveal a sinful struggle with the fear of man — fearing what people think rather than obeying what God says.
- Being controlled by the demands of expectation or significance could demonstrate a struggle with pride, wanting the glory for ourselves instead of humbly giving glory to God.
- Being driven by the demands of success could sink a pastor into an identity crisis that exposes pastoral ministry as an idol in his heart instead of finding his identity in Christ alone.

- Being consumed by the demands of friendship could lead to discontentment, emotional detachment from others, and a lack of trust in God's provision.

Every Christian, though forgiven and made new by the power of the gospel, must daily battle against their sinful flesh in this fallen world — and pastors are no different! In fact, I believe the Enemy specifically targets pastors, tempting us to turn our affections to something — someone — other than God, even good things like the ministry. This is a very real problem. A pastor can easily be deceived by his own sinful heart, even as he is deeply engaged in the rigors and sacrifices of pastoral ministry.

Yet there is hope not only that we can identify the sins that so easily entangle us and lead us to dishonor God and neglect our families, but also that we can overcome them. The same power of the gospel that has redeemed the sinful heart of every Christian pastor enables us to put off these sins and put on Christ. The gospel enables us to obey God's commands and answer Christ's calling to be faithful shepherds in our home and church. In the pages ahead, we will look at several biblical strategies for leveraging this restorative power against our broken, sinful hearts to find balance as we respond to the demands we face and learn to shepherd our families faithfully.

Discussion Questions

For a Wife to Ask Her Husband

1. To which of these demands are you most prone to succumb?
2. In what ways have these demands caused you to neglect our family?
3. What sinful desire do you identify in your heart that causes you to neglect our family?

For a Husband to Ask His Wife

1. Are you sometimes envious of the time I spend with our church, and how can we work on protecting our personal time?
2. Which demands do you struggle with? What are some ways I can help you overcome this struggle?
3. Are you or our family feeling neglected in any ways that I don't know about?

chapter 2

the solution

{brian}

It was the meeting I had been dreading. I was in eleventh grade, and things had not been going well with my current girlfriend. She requested a "define the relationship" talk. For those of you who have had to stomach these talks, you may be able to guess what happened next. We met, and the words I had been dreading to hear came out of her mouth. She wanted to break up with me and end the relationship. Hoping to ease the pain of rejection, she spoke those famous words: "Brian," she said, "it's not you — it's me!" (*Cara: Just for the record, I wasn't "the girl" requesting this talk.*)

"It's not you — it's me." Those simple words always have a deeper meaning. They are intended to cushion the blow to our pride and self-worth when we are rejected by someone we love. They are an attempt to place the blame on the person doing the rejecting, but the attempt, however noble it might be, always fails. In fact, the exact opposite happens. Hearing those five words can crush our spirit. We intuitively know the words are dishonest, that it's just a way of avoiding conflict and quickly ending an unhappy relationship.

Despite the overwhelmingly negative use of this phrase in most relationships, I want to suggest that for a pastor who is guilty of neglecting his family, this phrase is perhaps the most helpful place to begin. When a pastor owns the truth that "it's not _____; it's me," it becomes a helpful, honest starting point to deal with his neglect. In the previous chapter, we looked at how the pressures and demands a pastor faces can lead to misplaced priorities in his life. And though it is tempting to focus on the demands and blame them for our behavior, the root problem goes deeper. The problem rests not in the demands and pressures we face but in how we create idols out of those demands, idols that lead us to neglect our family and dishonor God. When we sinfully neglect our family, several consequences inevitably follow.

A pastor's neglect of his family reveals a disregard for several clear biblical imperatives, things that are commanded of every Christian husband and father (Ephesians 5:25–30; 6:4; 1 Peter 3:7). Additionally, neglect of his family reveals a disregard for the leadership qualification to "manage his own family well" (1 Timothy 3:4). These biblical imperatives reveal God's priority that a pastor should first shepherd and care for his family before his flock. Despite these clear expectations for leaders, their sinful responses to the demands of ministry lead many pastors to misplace their priorities. A Christian man's neglect of his family communicates that he does not value his family. Because the pastor is an example to his flock (1 Peter 5:3), he not only sets a bad example for the other Christian men in his congregation by his neglect, but even worse, a spirit of hypocrisy permeates his home. His wife and his children see the hypocrisy in his life. Pastoral disregard for the needs of their families is a leading cause of the clichéd disenchantment pastors' wives and their children sometimes have toward the church — and even toward Christ himself. The sins a pastor commits have consequences for himself, for his family, and for the church he serves.

{cara}

Wives, at times our husbands don't even know we are being neglected. Many women I know want their husbands to be mind readers. We want them to understand us so well that they will just know when things are wrong! But half the time we *don't even know what is wrong. The solution is not to beat them over the head with all the ways they fail, every time they walk through the door. At the same time, we should avoid bottling up our concerns and growing bitter and angry. We need to lovingly, wisely, and, above all, respectfully share our needs and the needs of our family, and then we must patiently pray for both our own heart and our husband's heart.*

Despite the serious consequences of neglecting his family, a pastor who succumbs to the demands and pressures of ministry at the expense of his family still has hope. There is power to overcome these sins and to rebuild what has been broken — the power of the gospel.[1] The same gospel that awakens a pastor's spiritually dead soul to life in Christ also has the power to bring victory over the burden of sins. Struggling pastors need to rely on two facets of the biblical gospel if they hope to experience its power: they need to own their sin, acknowledging their neglect and failure, and they need to rely on the grace Christ offers, trusting in the gifts and promises of God rather than in their own efforts to secure what they want and need.

Examine Your Heart

The first step a pastor must take in this process is to begin rebuilding that which has been harmed by neglect. This is where the power of the words "it's not you — it's me" is needed. A pastor should do what any follower of Jesus who struggles with sin must do — acknowledge his sin against God and against his family. He must confess his failure to God, and then to his wife and his children. He must confess that it is wrong to contend that his neglect is the result of the pressures he faces or the overwhelming demands on his time. These assertions can easily become excuses that hide the sin, justifications that keep him from true repentance. Some pastors' families may believe that the problems in their family lie with them. A husband who neglects his wife may find that she has begun to believe there is something wrong with her, that she is the reason her husband prefers to spend time with church members rather than quality time with her. A pastor's children may come to the reasonable assumption that their daddy loves the church more than them. To deal with the brokenness his neglect has created in his family, a pastor should begin by looking at his heart, owning what is truly sinful, confessing it to God and those he has sinned against, and repenting — turning away from the sinful patterns and choosing to follow God in faith and obedience.

Repentance is key to this process, not just to experience forgiveness with God, but also to experience restoration in our families by breaking neglectful patterns. Several years ago, I thought I was honestly acknowledging some sinful struggles and patterns of neglect to my wife and children, and I made some necessary changes in our family's schedule to reflect my commitment to break with my old habits and patterns. I will never forget the despair I felt a short time later when my wife confronted me and told me that very little change had actually taken place. She let me know that my children had especially noticed the lack of change. I realized that even though I had acknowledged my sin and confessed it to my family with the intention of making things better, my lack of substantial change revealed a lack of true repentance. When I truly repented, real and lasting change began to occur in my life.

Make no mistake, I still care for my family imperfectly. But my wife and children can now attest to the fruit of repentance in my life. The phone rarely gets answered during dinner and our devotional time as a family. I consistently seek to get home when I say I'm going to be home, not forty-five minutes to an hour later. For the past few years, I have used all of my allotted vacation time. Though every pastor will always remain a work in progress, it is possible by God's grace and the power of the gospel to break sinful patterns that have been established. Yet, without true repentance, little will change.

Put Off and Put On

Since repentance is essential, we must understand that biblical repentance involves more than confessing our sin and choosing not to do it any longer. The biblical model is "to put off your old self ... and to put on the new self" (Ephesians 4:22 – 24). In addition to putting off our sin, we must put on Christ; we must find positive patterns and habits to pursue and "put on" in place of our sinful patterns.

I have found four helpful biblical principles that a pastor can "put on" when he repents from his sin — all of which are rooted in God's design for the family. When applied, God can use these principles to break the patterns of neglect and reestablish healthy new patterns.

Remember the Biblical Qualifications

The apostle Paul outlines the qualifications of a pastor clearly in Scripture. A pastor (overseer, elder) is to be the faithful husband of one wife (1 Timothy 3:2; Titus 1:6) and a good manager of his children and household (1 Timothy 3:4–5; Titus 1:6). Paul's lists in both 1 Timothy 3 and Titus 1 are not exhaustive, but they contain several characteristics that can and should be observed and identified in any man aspiring to the office of a pastor (1 Timothy 3:1). These qualifications are also required of any pastor throughout his ministry. Keeping Paul's lists in our minds is a clear and helpful antidote to the problem of neglect. This divine standard helps pastors to remain aware of what is required of them to remain faithful to their family in the rigors of pastoral ministry. Ignoring this biblical standard inevitably leads to family neglect and often to disqualification from the pastoral office.

When the apostle Peter exhorted the elders (pastors) under his care to shepherd the flock of God (1 Peter 5:2), he called them to be "examples to the flock" (1 Peter 5:3). Peter had all aspects of life in mind, including the responsibility a man has to his wife and children. I once heard a seasoned pastor, Albert Martin, address a group of pastors with the topic of Christian marriage in view: "What does your church member do when a non-Christian walks through the door and asks them how a Christian man should treat his wife? You know what they should do? Point to you and say, 'Oh, just watch him. He's my pastor. You need to just watch the way he tenderly, lovingly, and sacrificially cherishes that woman next to him.'"

Pastors need to remember that God has established a high standard for those who shepherd his people in terms of how they live out their calling as a husband and father. As you put off your sin and put on Christ, remember that the fruit of God's work in your life, the things that first qualified you for pastoral ministry, must continue to be evident, not just to your church, but to your wife and children as well.

Let me add a necessary word of grace. You must never forget that the gifts you have for pastoral ministry are fruits of the gospel as well. They do not exist without the Spirit of God mightily at work in you and through you. Guard yourself against seeing these qualifications as a checklist to be accomplished in your own power and righteousness. Instead, turn to God in prayerful dependence, seeking these qualities as the spiritual fruit of God's gracious work in you. The gifts of God come through faith as you depend on Christ for your every need.

Love, Understand, and Delight in Your Wife

In the spirit of Peter's exhortation to be an example to the flock, it is also essential for pastors to keep before them God's design for marriage. God's redeeming design for marriage between a Christian husband and a Christian wife can be seen in Paul's commands to each of them in Ephesians. Wives are to submit to their husbands as they do to the Lord (Ephesians 5:22), and husbands are to love their wives as Christ loves the church and gave himself for her (Ephesians 5:25). This task is impossible for any Christian man to pursue if he does not make his wife a high priority, second only to Christ. How much more is this true for a pastor? How can a husband who neglects his wife and his family love his wife in a way that demonstrates to the rest of the flock the unconditional, sacrificial love of Christ?

Peter also communicates God's divine design for Christian marriage, but his approach differs somewhat from Paul's. Peter addresses the man who protests that his wife, like the church, is hard to love. He begins with instruction to Christian wives on how they are to obey Christ in dealing with a husband who is disobedient to the gospel message (1 Peter 3:1). They accomplish this by living a godly life before their disobedient husbands in the hope that their godly behavior will win over their husbands (1 Peter 3:2 – 4). With this background of a challenging marriage in mind, Peter next instructs Christian husbands: "Husbands, in the same way be considerate as you live with your wives, and treat them with respect as the weaker partner and as heirs with you of the gracious gift of life, so that nothing will hinder your prayers" (1 Peter 3:7).

Being considerate to your wife means understanding God's will for how a Christian husband should relate to his wife. This involves understanding and empathizing with your wife. A husband should be mindful of his wife's needs, struggles, and feelings. A pastor is also called to live with his wife in this way, not just as an example to his flock, but also because a pastor's wife faces unique challenges, demands, and pressures. These will demand his attentive care. An extra measure of steadfastness and faithfulness is necessary to make a pastor's wife feel cherished and honored. A pastor's wife may feel competition for her husband's affections in a way that other wives do not. She may have unique struggles and challenges that the wives of other men do not face. As a pastor and a husband, you will need to learn what these challenges are and how you can best serve your wife in love.

Although these imperatives for a Christian husband are helpful, biblical examples also help clarify what God expects. Consider Solomon's wise advice to his son in Proverbs 5. Solomon first warns his son about the adulterous woman — who she is and why he should stay far from her (Proverbs 5:1 – 14). Then in a stunning contrast, Solomon uses his vivid description of the adulterous woman to help his son realize why his delight should be solely in the wife of his youth (Proverbs 5:15 – 20). Solomon urges his son to delight sexually in his wife, not in the adulterous woman, by being "intoxicated with her love." Sacrificial love for your wife, loving her as Christ loved the church and living with her in an understanding way, should grow out of your delight in the wonderful, mysterious grace of God, the grace that has given this woman to you according to God's sovereign and wise plan.

Charles Spurgeon is often pegged as having been especially neglectful of his wife and two sons because he spent much of his time traveling around the world preaching. Yet even if we can find fault in some of his misplaced priorities, it is difficult to ignore the obvious delight Spurgeon had in his wife. This is especially true when we see the letters he wrote to her each day as he was traveling.[2] After Mrs. Spurgeon's appeal that he use his time to rest instead of write her so often, Charles Spurgeon responded with a letter that read, "Every word I write is a pleasure to me as much as ever it can be to you; it is only a lot of odds and ends I send you, but I put them down as they come, so that you may see it costs me no labor, but is just a happy scribble. Don't fret because I write you so many letters; it is such a pleasure to tell out my joy."[3] On another occasion, he sent her some pen and ink sketches he had drawn of the headdresses of Italian women, and he wrote, "Now, sweetheart, may these trifles amuse you; I count it a holy work to draw them, if they cause you but one happy smile."[4]

As they deal with their own demanding schedules and unexpected emergencies, pastors will do well to learn from Spurgeon's example. A pastor who truly delights in his wife needs to communicate that delight to her so she feels cherished by her husband. His goal is not just to observe the letter of the law; he should seek to be faithful to the intention behind these commands by cultivating a giddy delight in his wife and the intricacies of her personality. Ask God to make your wife grow more precious to you every day. *(Cara: Husbands, we don't expect much, really; we just want to feel important—and loved!)*

Shepherd, Train, and Instruct Your Children

The "elephant in the room" when we look at how pastors spend their time is the amount of time they actually spend instructing their own children. A pastor may spend several hours each week instructing and shepherding church members, but when he returns home, he will often take a more passive approach or rely on his wife to deal with the shepherding of their children. Sin blinds many pastors to this neglect of their children, and to combat it pastors must take to heart the clear biblical imperatives God gives to Christian fathers: "Fathers, do not exasperate your children; instead, bring them up in the training and instruction of the Lord" (Ephesians 6:4). There are many different ways in which Christian fathers can exasperate their children and provoke them to anger. A pastor's child who sees their father repeatedly choosing church responsibilities over spending time with them will eventually grow exasperated and may be provoked to anger. Children need to be shepherded and instructed in the Lord just as much as those a pastor is responsible for in the church.

But what does it look like for a Christian father to train and instruct his children in the Lord? In Deuteronomy, God spoke these words through his servant Moses:

> Hear, O Israel: The LORD our God, the LORD is one. Love the LORD your God with all your heart and with all your soul and with all your strength. These commandments that I give you today are to be on your hearts. Impress them on your children. Talk about them when you sit at home and when you walk along the road, when you lie down and when you get up. Tie them as symbols on your hands and bind them on your foreheads. Write them on the doorframes of your houses and on your gates.
>
> *Deuteronomy 6:4 – 9*

Three helpful principles can be found in God's words to those fathers who belonged to God's people, the Israelites. First, we should instruct and train our children so they can learn the truth about God and know what he expects from us (Deuteronomy 6:4 – 5). There is a purpose to what we teach, a desire to see our children know God and believe and accept the gospel. Second, we instruct our children using God's Word so the Scriptures transform our children's hearts (Deuteronomy 6:6 – 7). The Bible is the source of what we teach and the final authority for our lives. Finally, we should instruct our children in our homes, not just relying on gatherings in the church, so God's Word becomes the central focus of our home (Deuteronomy 6:8 – 9). We should teach regularly as part of our daily family life together. Pastors need to establish priorities in this regard, committing first to instruct their own children in the Lord and then seeking to instruct the church.

{cara}

Wives, we play a very important role in this process. We need to encourage our husbands as they do this. One way to do so is by giving up some of our time with our husbands so they can spend that time, perhaps one-on-one, with the children. Our children are only home for a short time, so it's important that we make this a priority.

Second, we need to remember that we are the ones who spend the most time with our children. As a homeschooling mom, I spend most of my day with the kids. I see firsthand their struggles and the ways they are growing. I need to share these things with my husband so he knows how to wisely train and instruct our children. I shouldn't expect him to magically know what has happened throughout the day or to know the specific needs of our children. As husband and wife, we are in this together, so we need to work together.

Finally, we need to encourage our children to desire time with their dads, and yet we should teach them to be gracious when unexpected things call their dad away. We do this best by our own example. We should be excited to see our husbands when they come home, and we need to be gracious and understanding when the church needs him.

Embrace Your Call to Give an Account

Perhaps the most sobering truth for a pastor comes from the author of Hebrews: "Have confidence in your leaders and submit to their authority, because they keep watch over you as *those who must give an account*. Do this so that their work will be a joy, not a burden, for that would be of no benefit to you" (Hebrews 13:17, emphasis added). Even though this particular instruction is given to all Christians, it holds a penetrating truth for pastors and church leaders. The clear implication of this word from the author of Hebrews is that pastors will give an account for their work of shepherding others. One day, they will answer to the Chief Shepherd.

I remember the immense pressure I felt when I took my first senior pastor position and realized I would have to give an account to God for the way I pastored and cared for all of these people. I would lie in bed at night, unable to sleep because of this burden. Not long afterward, I realized I was focusing so much on my responsibility to the church that I had forgotten about an equally important responsibility — my care for my own family. I asked myself this question: If I will someday give an account for the way I have cared for the people in our church, how much more of an account must I give for the souls of those in my home? Sadly, some pastors spend their entire life in ministry focused on caring for their church members while ignoring the care of those living under their own roofs.

There is much at stake here. The consequences of these sins of neglect can be disastrous. Yet thanks be to God! We have a great Savior who has not only purchased for us forgiveness from our sins and salvation from the wrath to come but has freed us from the bondage of our sin. Those who have been commissioned by the Chief Shepherd should know the reality of this freedom more than anyone. We must first examine our hearts, confessing our sins to God and to our family and truly repenting of our neglect and disobedience as fathers and husbands. We must put on Christ and commit to doing what he has clearly commanded us to do — modeling what it means to be a godly father and husband for our flock.

Discussion Questions

For a Pastor—Asked by Fellow Pastors or Other Mature Christians

1. Have you ever acknowledged and confessed your neglect of your family to God and your family? What, specifically, do you need to confess?
2. What have been some of the consequences of that neglect?
3. In what areas do you believe you most need to grow as a father and husband? How do you think your wife would answer that question? Your children?
4. If you had to give an account to God for the way you have shepherded your family today, what would you say? How does the gospel motivate you to shepherd your family with grace and love?

Reflection

Signs of Grace in Ministry

Jim Savastio

An older writer once remarked that "the life of the minister is the life of his ministry." When the Bible gives us the qualifications for pastoral ministry, it repeatedly highlights the importance of a man's character and his relationships with others—especially his family relationships. By the grace of God, I have enjoyed the dual joys of marriage and ministry for over twenty years now. I was married just before the start of my last year of seminary, so my wife and I have known little-to-nothing of married life apart from our life in ministry together. All of my children have been born and raised in the midst of their dad's pastoral labors. Yet despite the challenges of pastoral ministry, our lives have been blessed by God, a blessing I attribute to several ways in which God's grace has been especially evident to me.

1. God's grace has been evident through the blessing of *bad examples.* I tend to learn more from my failures than from my successes in ministry, and I am deeply affected by the warnings I receive from others. I've learned what to avoid from those who have made a shipwreck of their families. When a motorist sees a car spinning out on the ice in front of him, he can take action to stop, slow down, or take an alternate route. In the same way, a man can learn to avoid some of the worst mistakes in his ministry and family life by recognizing and avoiding the mistakes others have made.

2. Along with the warnings of bad examples, I've also seen God's grace through the blessing of *good examples.* When God saved me, he placed me in a fellowship where I saw a godly pastor interacting graciously with his wife and children. I saw the men of the church loving and serving their wives, lovingly instructing and disciplining their children. I saw happy homes, filled with joy. Look around you and seek out good examples. Ask these men what they do and learn from them.

3. The third sign of God's grace has been through the blessing of *good instruction*. When I was training for the ministry, one of my mentors repeatedly reminded me that my calling as a pastor would never negate my calling as a Christian man to love and care for my family. As a young believer I was clearly taught the biblical passages concerning marriage and the family. The truth of these foundational principles of God's Word were vividly vindicated in the lives of men who embraced or turned from God's truth. If you don't fully understand what it means to be a godly husband and father, study the Scriptures and learn from good, godly teachers.

4. I've known God's grace through the blessing of a *praying and supportive wife*. My wife has always been supportive of my ministry. As Cara has pointed out, it is a pastor's wife who most often bears the burden of a sudden emergency or a call in the middle of the night. How a wife deals with these realities will powerfully affect the health and well-being of the family. A wise pastor will not ignore his wife, knowing that her prayer and support are integral to the long-term health of his ministry.

5. Finally, I've been blessed by the support of a *well-instructed flock—our church*. I am blessed to serve a church that faithfully prays for my family and supports me in making my wife and children a priority in my life. The church has never complained when I dedicate nights to being with our family at home, spend time playing with my children on the ball field, or take time away from my ministry responsibilities for a family vacation. They let my wife simply be my wife and do not treat her as an unpaid staff member. They avoid putting my kids in the proverbial "fishbowl," and they protect them from the overwhelming expectations that turn many pastors' children against the church.

These are just a few of the blessings of God's grace that have given me the dual joys of a happy pastorate and a happy family.

Jim Savastio has pastored for twenty-five years and is currently involved in training young pastors.

part 2

the pastor's wife

"I Don't Recall Saying 'I Do' to This!"

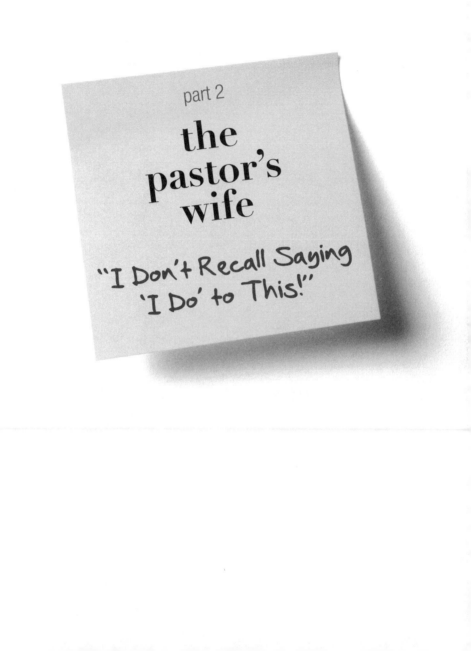

chapter 3

the struggle

{cara}

Life as a pastor's wife has not been an easy road for me to travel. There have been challenges, frustrations, and great pain along the way. I recall an eight-month period recently when my family and our church experienced tremendous loss. We buried a beloved church member who was one month shy of her 107th birthday; lost two of our close friends (a pastor and his wife), who were both killed in a car accident; and then three days later lost one of our young deacons. Tragically, he too was killed in a car accident, leaving behind his wife and two young children. While attending his funeral, we learned of the death of another of our deacons who had served the church faithfully for over fifty years. We buried a faithful church member who lost his battle with cancer and then buried my uncle after he committed suicide. In eight short months, we experienced the deaths of seven people we loved — people we were close to in our family and in ministry, people we cared for, people who had served and supported us. In the midst of all this, two of my closest friends left our church (their husbands were called to pastor other churches).

It was hard.

Dealing with the challenges of life itself can be hard. But when you add the unique relationships a pastor and his wife develop with those they shepherd, dealing with loss and pain can be even more difficult. It is a hardship for our husbands. And it is hard on us as their wives.

Ministry is a way of life that requires us to constantly pour ourselves out for others, giving sacrificially of our time, resources, and emotions. It is a life that demands selflessness as we serve others. And if we are not careful, it can leave us empty, discouraged, and broken. But there are many joys and rewards as well. Even in the midst of challenge and heartache, we see the grace of God at work and gain a front-row seat to the amazing miracle of God's love ministering to the people we care for and shepherd.

Dealing with Unrealistic Expectations

Sure, I can work in the nursery and be in the worship service at the same time.

Churches often place unrealistic expectations on pastors and their wives. If you are a pastor's wife, you've probably felt this. Sometimes we put these expectations on ourselves, or our husbands place them on us. However they get there, we need to deal with these expectations and respond in healthy, God-honoring ways.

People in your church may expect you to lead the children's ministry; be at every church event; attend every worship service, baby shower, funeral, and wedding; and then have your home open 24/7 to provide meals, host missionaries, and lead small groups. On top of the expectations that have to do with your ministry and service for the church, there are expectations for how we choose to dress, raise our children, and address our husbands in public. The list of expectations is endless — and constantly changing. As a pastor's wife, you can't escape these expectations, and you can't pretend they don't exist. So what *can* you do? You must learn to face them head-on and deal with them.

A wise pastor's wife once told me that the wife of a pastor should be seen, but that doesn't mean we have to "do it all." In other words, it's important that the wife of a pastor shares his desire to serve the church, but her service cannot be motivated by a concern for what other people think. Instead, we must learn from the truth of God's Word. I often turn to Titus 2, where God gives us a list of the responsibilities of a woman of God:

> Likewise, teach the older women to be reverent in the way they live, not to be slanderers or addicted to much wine, but to teach what is good. Then they can urge the younger women to love their husbands and children, to be self-controlled and pure, to be busy at home, to be kind, and to be subject to their husbands, so that no one will malign the word of God.
>
> *Titus 2:3 – 5*

I know of several terrific books that explore the life and example of the woman described in Titus 2, so I won't repeat what is said there.[1] It is important to note, however, that among all of the expectations mentioned in this passage, there is nothing that addresses how many hours you need to serve in the nursery or how many meetings you need to host in your home. An important aspect of

Titus 2 is focused on how a wife and mother can serve and love her family with the right heart and attitude. This passage gives the motivation for our actions as well, stressing the importance of setting a God-honoring example for others ("so that no one will malign the word of God"). There is nothing specifically addressing the degree to which you must be involved in the church. This means that any expectations you sense in this area are likely rooted in something other than Scripture.

It is important for the wife of a pastor to consider her role as a helpmate to her husband and how this impacts their life in the home and in their ministry together. The best place to start is by talking with your husband and asking for his wisdom and guidance in this area. That's right, ladies — whether we like it or not, we need our husbands and their wise leadership in this area of our life. We need to allow them to lead us, and we should encourage them by asking for their guidance. Each marriage and each ministry calling are unique, and each husband's needs are unique, so it is impossible to outline specific measures for your particular situation. I hope your husband knows your gifting and your limitations and how your gifts, personality, and unique insights can best help him in ministering to the church you've been called to serve.

As you begin this discussion, you may feel your husband thinks you can do more than you actually can. You may need to have some honest conversations about what it really takes to host people in your home — the actual work involved in doing this. But the key here is that you are communicating about these expectations. As your husband understands more of what is involved with your schedule and as you take the time to express your feelings of being overwhelmed, you may find that his expectations will change to accommodate your needs as he seeks to serve you in love. And what if he thinks you truly can do more, even if you don't think you can? Guess what, ladies! The truth is that God is bigger than what we think we can do! As you share your honest concerns and make known your feelings of being overwhelmed, you may still find yourself challenged to grow and do things you don't feel comfortable doing. Such times are great reminders that God is the one who gives us the strength and energy we need to do what is necessary. By God's strength, we can get through the hard times, and he grants us the rest we need to accomplish all that he sets before us.

{brian}

Brothers, when your wife shares her concerns and says she feels overwhelmed by your expectations, listen to her. We need to be mindful of the pressures we place on our wives. As we determine how much to ask of them, we have to consider the unique pressures they face each day. Pastors are notorious for seeing the needs of the church more clearly than our own wife's need for help. Guard against piling too much on your wife. Take time to understand what her day is like. Get familiar with the work she does in caring for the family and ministering in the church.

Struggling with Loneliness

Will you be my friend? Why not?!

I've never met the president of the United States. We've never spoken. But I imagine I have at least one thing in common with him (and likely his wife as well). There are many people who want to know us, many who feel like they do know us, and a whole lot of people who want our counsel and advice — but there are very, very few people who actually "know" who we really are. Pastors and their wives serve others and have a very public role in the community, but their own personal relationships can be overlooked and neglected. You may have people in your life who feel close to you, but you may not share that same sense of closeness with them. You may be aware of many of the intimate details of their lives, but your own life is a closed book to them.

Whatever the reasons behind this, it's hard to escape the fact that being a pastor's wife can be very lonely. You may be lonely because your church is small and the members disagree with or dislike your husband. You may be in a large church where everyone assumes you have many friends. You may be a stay-at-home mom in a church full of working women, or a working woman in a church full of stay-at-home moms. Perhaps you have opened up in the past and have been betrayed or wounded and are now scared to be vulnerable again.

When my husband and I first married, we served in a small country church where my husband was the youth pastor. I was twenty years old, and the majority of the church members were either much older than I was (many were old enough to be my parents) or young enough for me to babysit them. Needless to say, some of my loneliness was due to the fact that I was so young and new to both marriage and ministry. I struggled with loneliness for the entire time we were there.

My struggle with loneliness did not improve when we moved to a new church. I found that we faced obstacles at every church we served. It didn't matter if my husband was a youth pastor, an associate pastor, or a senior pastor. In fact, as a senior pastor's wife now, I have found that some women are intimidated by my position. Something prevents them from approaching me, and I'm not sure how to overcome that barrier.

I remember one day when I went to lunch with one of our church members. Her husband was getting ready to accept a senior pastor position. She had lots of questions for me. At one point during our time together, she commented that she was surprised she hadn't been invited to many homes for lunch. She had assumed that people would want to get to know her better. I chuckled and asked her to guess how many homes I had been invited to go to for lunch. She was shocked at my answer. Her assumption, which I find to be fairly common, is that a pastor and his wife are regularly accepting invitations to lunches and events. But the truth is that I hadn't been invited to more than a handful of homes. This isn't necessarily true of every church, and our current church is a notable exception to this trend, caring wonderfully for our family and for me as an individual. Still, my experience has taught me that if I sit back and wait for others to take the initiative in building relationships, I will remain quite lonely.

I'm not an extrovert. I'd be perfectly content sitting in the corner of the sanctuary and watching others. And the fact that I'm an introvert makes it even harder for me to build friendships with the women of our church. But as a pastor's wife, I've learned that I need to take the first step and approach the women in our church. I must be deliberate in making relationships and work hard to sustain them.

We also need to cry out to God. Our loneliness may be self-inflicted, but it may also be true that God has not yet provided us with a friend for this season of our life. We must learn to be content with the grace God gives us and deepen our relationship with God during our times of loneliness. The truth is that he is a close companion, a perfect friend, and one who sticks closer than a brother. God is all-compassionate, all-knowing, and all-present. If Christ is not sufficient for us, then no relationship on earth will be able to meet our need.

Finally, we must be patient. Deep, lasting friendships are not built overnight. They take time and investment. They take patience, honesty, vulnerability, and forgiveness. And you may not have many of them. It's not unusual to only have one or two really close friends. We need to recognize these friendships as a kind gift from God, thanking him, even if it's just for that one person he has provided, rather than lamenting our lack of close relationships.

Overlooked, Yet Looked Over

Being invisible — unless there is a problem!

Brian and I had been at our current church for just a few months. One Sunday morning during the greeting time, a deacon came up to me and pointed to the associate pastor's wife. "Carla," he said, "what is that lady's name? I don't want to get it wrong." In case you missed the irony of his question, my name is not Carla — it's Cara! An honest mistake, to be sure; yet, even though I can laugh now, at the time his blunder was very hurtful to me. My husband had been pastoring the church for several months, and one of the key leaders in the church still didn't know my name. I felt overlooked and unimportant. (For the record, this deacon *does* know my name now, and he warmly greets me every Sunday morning.)

Being overlooked and feeling unimportant go hand in hand with the struggle a pastor's wife has with loneliness. Your role as a wife is lived out in the shadow of your husband. You are seen by many, yet at the same time you are invisible. Whenever I greet someone who is new to our church, I debate in my head whether I should let them know that I am the pastor's wife. It's not that I'm ashamed or embarrassed — far from it! But I know that once they know who my husband is, *who I am* will be secondary. There are times when I want them to get to know me first as Cara, a unique person, and then as Cara, the pastor's wife.

For those of us who are pastors' wives, our husbands' ministries are public and visible. They are in front of the people, preaching and teaching. While this is happening, we are often in the nursery or in the pews trying to keep our children quiet. While our husbands are out meeting and fellowshipping with other members, we are often stuck at home with sick kids! Our needs and our contributions to the family and to the church tend to get overlooked. Sometimes we are hesitant to even let people know we have needs in the first place.

Rarely, if ever, will I hear a church member thank me for caring for my family so my husband is free and available to minister to others. Ironically, we are more likely to hear about all the issues that people want us to communicate to our husbands. Whenever there is a criticism, we are suddenly noticed, as if we have any control over the topic at hand! We can suddenly go from being invisible to feeling like we are living under a microscope. I remember when our third daughter was born. We had been at the church for six months, and I was a nursing mom with a four-year-old and a two-year-old. I frequently had to get up during the service to feed the baby, and several people criticized me for doing this. I learned the hard way that everything I did was seen and noticed by church members — they were clearly watching me — yet my personal needs remained invisible and unmet.

There is no simple solution to this tension of having every action seen by others while your personal needs remain invisible. The best solution is to remember that we do not serve for human approval or praise (Galatians 1:10). In addition, we need to find a voice and begin to communicate our needs to others. Honestly, I am terrible at this. I tend to think I can do everything on my own. Whenever I fall into this way of living, God quickly reminds me that I cannot do it all by myself. I am reminded that I need him first and foremost, but I also need others as well. This means we are willing to speak up and share when we have a need. A pastor's wife needs to set an example for the women in the church, showing others that we are not self-sufficient. We must learn to humble ourselves and ask for help.

This may be as simple as asking someone to pray for us. As we were writing this book, a close friend wondered how many people we had asked to pray for us and our writing project. I was immediately convicted that I had not asked a single person to pray for me. I was relying on myself, doing it all on my own. Her reminder was gentle and firm, and it was necessary. It helped me think through my needs and identify those I should be asking to support me in prayer. If we do not make our needs known to others, we cannot expect them to help us.

Learning to Handle Criticism

Are you talking to me?

Dealing with criticism has been one of my greatest challenges. But it's not criticism of me that is hard — it's when people criticize my husband and my children. It is very difficult for a wife to watch her husband faithfully slaving over his sermon preparation, only to have several church members tell him (or mention to you) that he preaches far too long. It hurts to watch him praying and fasting over important decisions and then hear from someone that they don't trust his leadership and feel he is taking the church in the wrong direction. It feels like a betrayal when, after watching him invest countless hours in discipling a young man, that person then questions whether or not your husband should even be in ministry. Sadly, these aren't just examples I've made up. All of this has happened at some point in Brian's pastoral ministry.

When our husbands grow discouraged, we must help them pick up the pieces. It's an extremely important job — helping them sift through criticism to see if there is any truth to the accusations, providing a balanced perspective, and then encouraging them as they seek to forgive and love people again. A pastor's wife plays an essential role during these crucial moments. I have known wives who have greatly influenced their husbands' responses to criticism, either positively or negatively. A wife can encourage her husband to respond with graciousness, humility, godliness, and forgiveness, or she can influence her husband toward bitterness, anger, hatred, pride, and revenge. The way a wife responds to her husband requires prayer, great wisdom, and extreme caution. For some, this means learning to guard their tongue, taking time to develop a humble and forgiving spirit.

One of the most common temptations you will face is to take everything personally. We can easily become blinded and forget that we need to sift what is said. Some of the most difficult conversations I've had with my husband centered on helping him sort through criticism. There is usually a grain of truth somewhere in the criticism, something both of us can learn from. We don't want us to miss these occasions to learn and grow, and we don't want our husbands to overlook opportunities to develop in ways that will make them better pastors. Instead of seeking to justify his response, a wife needs to encourage her husband by acknowledging his God-given leadership abilities. She needs to bless him in the ways in which he is leading faithfully and shepherding well. She needs to encourage him to seek God and to learn from any valid criticism that can lead to change and to resist those that are personal attacks.

A seasoned pastor's wife once gave me some advice. She said we must remember that our battle is not against flesh and blood — it's a spiritual battle. I've often been reminded of this truth in the midst of intense seasons of difficulty and criticism. Knowing where the real battle lies has given me the ability to forgive the offenses of others and to remember the bigger picture — that we are not just seeking to win arguments or prove ourselves right; we are fighting a spiritual battle for the hearts and minds of people.

We need to be aware of how much we can handle and then clearly communicate this to our husbands. I recall some of the early years in ministry when we had a few particularly vicious members' meetings. I found it difficult to sit through these meetings and not say a word. Our children were also getting old enough to understand a bit of what was happening. To protect myself and my children, I began working in the nursery during these meetings. I found that skipping the actual meeting and then talking it out with my husband afterward was much easier, and I wasn't so emotionally charged. This helped me to be a more helpful and objective listener for him. The key is to know yourself — what your areas of weakness are and what you can and cannot handle.

{brian}

Pastors, we throw a major kink in the process of sifting through criticisms when we do not listen to our wives. Your wife can be your greatest asset to help you learn and grow through some harsh times, if you will only listen to her and give her the freedom to speak honestly to you.

A Demanding Schedule

There is a church cookout — this *weekend?! Why didn't you mention this last week?*

My husband's father is a family practice doctor, and for several years I worked for his practice. Doing this job helped me understand what a demanding schedule he and his fellow colleagues had as doctors. Often, they had to be at the hospital for hours before their office opened, and they would spend countless hours after the office closed returning calls and answering emergency calls from patients. Vacations were few and far between. There were no "regular" hours for them. They had to make sacrifices in their personal lives to care for their patients, and they made these sacrifices without complaining. They knew this was the life they had chosen, and their patients were grateful for their sacrifices.

I have found that life in full-time pastoral ministry isn't much different from life in medicine. My family doctor and I have often commiserated together when we discussed the similarities between our lives and the chaotic family schedules we manage. The truth is that most church members only see our husbands preaching on Sunday mornings (possibly evenings) and then teaching again on Wednesday nights. But we know there is more to being a pastor than teaching and preaching a few times a week! We know they spend many hours preparing sermons and lessons. We know about the people who want to meet our husbands for counsel or coffee. We know about the calls they get in the middle of the night. I wish I had a way of counting the number of times I've heard someone say, "Pastor, I know this is your day off, but..."

Pastors don't really have a "day off." The truth that no one tells you but everyone knows is that there are no "regular" hours for a pastor's family. Sure, we try to have a regular schedule, but the reality is that life doesn't follow a regular schedule. Have you ever tried to plan when a person has to go to the emergency room or is in a car accident? Or when a baby is born or someone has a marital crisis?

Given that it is virtually impossible to predict and plan a regular schedule, what can you do to maintain some semblance of normal family life together? First, and most important, try to be gracious when your husband has to respond to the needs of others. There are many nights after my husband comes home following a long day of writing sermons and counseling people when the phone rings, and he has to head to the hospital or visit someone in need. He does not choose this! Trust me, he would much rather stay home and enjoy time with his family. In fact, he would rather give the kids a bath or take the dog for a walk, but he also knows the church needs him — and they need him now! He deeply loves our people, and the Lord always gives strength to minister to them.

When these crisis situations occur, I have a choice to make. I can choose to graciously allow him the freedom to minister, or I can choose to be bitter and angry that I must give up my time with my husband and do our parenting tasks alone. I don't always respond perfectly in these moments. Some nights I sit by myself and feel very lonely because I haven't seen or talked to my husband all day. But I find it helpful to remember that this isn't ideal for him either. Both of us have been called to this life. Being available to serve others in need is an inherent aspect of pastoral ministry.

So we begin by acknowledging that there is a level of discomfort and pain in being a pastor's wife. That's why we need to be gracious and understanding. But we must also be sure to remind our husbands of our needs and the needs of the children as well. Pastors struggle with balancing their priorities, and they can sometimes fall into patterns that reflect misplaced priorities. Sinful habits and idols sometimes lead a pastor to focus too much of his time and energy on the needs of the church to the point of neglecting his family. As pastors' wives, we should prayerfully and graciously inform our husbands of our needs and give them specific ways they can care for us. We can help by coming up with reasonable and manageable schedules for the family.

I remember asking the wife of a pastor who had served for more than forty years in ministry, "As you think about the struggles pastors' wives face in their marriage and ministry, what is the single biggest struggle you see today?" Her response surprised me. Her sense was that, compared to previous generations, men today tend to be more helpful around the house and more involved with the children, yet wives seem to have even higher expectations! I took her honest assessment to heart and saw my own generation reflected in her words. In light of her words, I offer some suggestions to consider before you approach your husband to talk about the "schedule."

Begin by assessing a few things. First, is what I am asking of my husband reasonable? Second, is there another way to accomplish what I desire outside of asking my husband? Third, is this what is most helpful for our family? Fourth, is how we are spending our time right now most honoring to God? It is essential that you talk to your husband about what is realistic for your schedule as a family. Discuss how many people typically come to visit your home in a month. Talk over how much vacation time he takes and when you can have intentional family time. And above all, make sure your requests are reasonable and realistic.

Confidentiality Matters

They said what to whom?

You do not need to know everything your husband does in his work and ministry. In fact, there are many things he *should not* share with you to protect the confidentiality of others. It is not our business to know the dirt on each and every church member, nor is it our job to be involved in offering counsel for every situation. Yet there will be times when our husbands need to share things with us, when they seek our advice on how to advise a particular member. Our life experiences may make us uniquely suited for helping another church member. But when confidential details are shared and our opinion is sought, we need to give our counsel with much fear and trembling. As our knowledge of others increases, so will the temptation to want to share that information with other people.

I realize not every woman is tempted to gossip, but at the very least, we should be aware that the biblical warning to older women not to be "malicious gossips" (Titus 2:3 NASB) is there for a very good reason! Whether we are young or old, we need to be deliberate about guarding our tongues. We should not demand information from our husbands that they are not free to tell us. Even if they are free to share, we should trust their judgment. My husband is very cautious about the information he shares with me, particularly if it involves other men in our church. For example, knowing which men in our church are struggling with pornography is neither necessary nor helpful for me to know. It can even be harmful. If I demand that my husband share what he knows, I place him in a difficult position. In some cases, sharing information with me may constitute a breach of confidentiality and can have legal consequences as well.

The truth is that we may not be able to handle all of the information that is shared. Our husbands must be able to trust that we are not going to turn around and tell our best friend all that we have been told. Sharing any confidential information, even as a prayer request, is still a breach of trust, a form of sinful gossip. If we cannot be trusted with confidential information, then we should not be told that information. If a pastor's wife wishes to be involved in giving counsel to her husband, she should seek to develop control over her tongue and avoid gossip.

Is it ever helpful for a pastor to share information with his wife? My husband has involved me in several counseling situations with women at our church, both as a protection for him and because in some situations I can relate to and understand what is going on better than he can. He has been very deliberate about meetings with women, setting up a standard where he does not meet with women alone. Because of this, I trust that my husband will avoid compromising situations, and he is always quick to involve me if it looks as though there may even be a hint of uncertainty or something questionable. He also knows he can trust me in these situations, and, more important, the people of our church know I can be trusted. When asked, I am clear that I will not share any information without receiving permission from that person, and I usually don't even ask to share information unless I discern a good reason they might want it shared. As wives of church leaders, our actions can have grave consequences.

{brian}

Pastors, we must lead our wives well to capture a fruitful balance when it comes to sharing information. Stray too far to one side, and we are keeping our heart from our wives and cutting them out of our inner circle; stray too far to the other side, and they can feel trapped about situations in which they have no voice or recourse. The most important thing to remember in finding this balance is that she is your wife, not your fellow pastor. Include her for her benefit and the benefit of others, but she is not called or required to carry the same burdens you are.

You Don't Have to Be a Theological Giant

"The necessary reformation of an eschatologically sanctified puritanical person." Yes, I know that didn't make sense — that's my point!

I will occasionally break out in a cold sweat during a Sunday school class when a question is addressed to me. It might be a question about a sermon that, for the life of me, I cannot remember. Sometimes, it's a theological question that contains words with so many syllables that it feels like the person asking is speaking a foreign language. I confess that I don't always understand the conversations our seminary students have, nor do I get all of their jokes. But they seem to assume that I do! I smile and laugh along, but inside I'm thinking to myself, "I have absolutely no idea what you just said."

It's important for women to be in the Bible, learning the Scriptures. We need to study God's Word, but we do not have to be theological giants just because we are married to a pastor. If you have a strong desire to study, I bless and encourage that. Learn the overall picture of the Bible. Know the gospel. Studying theology is important, but just knowing and understanding the jargon of theology won't matter all that much. I'll be the first to admit I'd rather read Jane Austen's *Pride and Prejudice* than Wayne Grudem's *Systematic Theology* or D. A. Carson's *Exegetical Fallacies.* When we lie in bed at night reading, I will be lost in the world of Mr. Darcy while my husband is trying to decipher the theological implications of the Holocaust and consider the problem of evil.

For some reason, people in our church tend to assume that if my husband knows the theological answer to a question, then I must know it too. But the truth is that we have some women in our church who are far more knowledgeable about theological matters than I am. So what do you do when someone asks you, "How is your soteriology formed by your convictions about the doctrine of predestination?" I'll tell you what I would say. I'd look them in the eye, cross my arms, and say, "No hablo seminary." Seriously, admitting that we do not always know the answer is more than acceptable. It is entirely appropriate to defer to your husband and other pastors on the deeper questions of theology. It takes humility to admit that we don't know something. Admitting that we do not know everything makes us human, approachable, and a whole lot less intimidating. When I tell a woman, "I don't know; let's go ask Brian about that," I often see her breathe a sigh of relief. It is almost as if she is relieved to find out that she isn't as stupid as she feels, that she is not alone in not understanding something.

At the same time, while we should admit we don't know it all, we should also be eager to study and search for an answer. We should not be so intimidated by the world of theology that we don't engage with it at all. In the process of studying, we will inevitably learn and grow. We may end up learning some of the lingo and grow to enjoy the world of theological discussion.

Avoid the Stereotypes

No, I don't play the piano and weave baskets.

When Brian told me he wanted to become a senior pastor, I really struggled with the idea. It wasn't because I doubted his gifts or his calling; it was because I didn't think I fit the stereotype of a pastor's wife. I just knew there was *no way* God would ever want me to be in that role. I assumed that a pastor's wife was the woman who played the piano every Sunday, sang in the choir, headed up Vacation Bible School, weaved baskets, and sewed quilts. And I knew I didn't do any of those things. I tried to sew once. I was determined to make curtains for our dining room. So I picked out the perfect fabric and found a woman who agreed to teach me how to sew them. About two hours into the project, she assigned me the job of ironing. She quickly realized I possessed no gifts in the area of sewing — but I can iron really well!

The truth is that we all have preconceived ideas, some positive and some negative, of what a pastor's wife should be. These ideas feed into the existing expectations we place on ourselves, as well as into the ones placed on us by the church. We need to remember that each ministry is unique and each marriage is unique, and God has uniquely gifted us for the position and role we are in.

God does not place us somewhere without equipping us to function in the role to which he has called us. He promises to give us help in our time of need (Hebrews 4:16). I know God has given me the ability to be the wife my husband needs me to be. I know I am gifted to serve the needs of our church in a way that is unique to who I am. How I am gifted may be very different from how you are gifted, and that's OK. We are each called to serve in the role God has placed us in.

We are also in different stages of life, and our ability and availability to serve may change as we grow older. Now that our youngest is five years old, I can do things that I couldn't do when we had kids under the age of five. And when I'm an empty nester and our kids are gone from our home, I will be able to do things I cannot do now. Our ministry will change over time as we go through different phases of our lives. No two pastors' wives' ministries will ever look the same.

Sewing for a ministry or baking bread for church members can be wonderful ways to serve your church, but you do not have to sew or bake to be a fruitful pastor's wife. While you may be gifted to play the piano and sing in the choir, I may be gifted to lead a small group. We are more than just a stereotype; we are unique women of God, distinctly gifted for our husbands and our churches.

Fight the Spiritual Battle

Some days I think I need body armor — but I really need God's armor!

Earlier, I shared helpful advice from a seasoned pastor's wife, a reminder that our battle is against more than just flesh and blood.

We fight a spiritual battle, and the longer we are in ministry, the more intensely we will feel this battle waging around us. It is a relentless fight that rages on day and night.

And it is very real. We are involved in doing life-changing work that has eternal implications. We are responsible for encouraging people to seek God in every aspect of their lives. We must combat negative messages and attacks from Satan himself, and he is not happy about this. Ignoring the battle is akin to going through life half blind. There are times when I see the battle clearly. Maybe there are conflicts in our church; no one seems to get along; marriages are falling apart; we are stretched thin and become discouraged. In times like these, Satan tempts us by questioning whether we are truly meant to be in this position, whether the work is worth it, whether any of it really matters.

I struggle greatly with depression. In the back of this book, I've included a small entry discussing some of my struggle, but at this point let me just say that the mental battle I must engage in on a daily basis is both discouraging and exhausting. I know that part of this battle is the result of Satan targeting me where I am most vulnerable. Because of Satan's constant attacks, I have to know my weaknesses well and proactively seek God and his Word to combat those thoughts.

As the wife of a pastor, you must be on guard. You need to know yourself well enough to know where you are vulnerable and take steps to put on your armor and fight. You also need to know your husband well enough to know where he is vulnerable, and you need to be praying daily for him, for yourself, and for your children. You need to be in God's Word and feeding on it. And you need to include others in the battle as well. Some of my biggest allies have been my husband and my friends. They are the ones who remind me that my struggles are not just against the flesh but against Satan himself. They are also the ones who join me in praying for my family and myself.

{brian}

The spiritual battle against the Enemy for a pastor and his family is intense. The front lines of gospel ministry invite attack. I know it. You know it. And yet, I have a confession to make: I often forget this! Not only do I forget the spiritual battle; I blindly conclude that the struggles and discouragements I experience are anything but the attacks of the Enemy. This denial creates two challenges: it keeps me from discerning what is happening when I am attacked and how best to face it, and it limits my ability to lead and shepherd my family through these attacks. The best way to deal with these intense attacks is to remember they exist and prepare yourself in advance. Remember that the Enemy prowls around like a lion looking for someone to devour. Christians are never exempt from these attacks. How much more is this true for a pastor? And yet, we must remember that greater is he who is in us than he who is in the world. The power of Christ is present and available to those who will take up the full armor of God and do battle, knowing that the victory is ours in Christ.

We cannot go into this battle unarmed, yet many of us do so. We tend to be reactive instead of proactive. A game cannot be won on defense alone! But there is good news for us: we are not in this battle alone. In fact, the battle has already been won for us through the cross and resurrection of Christ. Though we participate in the battle, we fight a defeated foe.

The Joys of Being a Pastor's Wife

Most of this chapter has been spent focusing on the struggles of being a pastor's wife. But I don't want to end there, for this role has many joys as well. What are some of them? First of all, we are married to a pastor! Yes, I know this may sound obvious, but it can bring about deep joy. We are married to someone who is doubly responsible for caring for our souls, and we get the joy and blessing of ministering to one of God's chosen servants in a unique and personal way. We provide a place of refuge and rest for these men of God. We get to encourage them in their work, glean from their knowledge, and experience their care firsthand. We encourage them both with our words and by being physically intimate with them. Don't underestimate the temptations that pastors face from adulterous women. Satan knows there is no quicker way to ruin the fruitful ministry of a pastor than infidelity. We help provide protection from this sin by being available mentally, emotionally, and physically for our husbands.

We have the privilege of serving the servants. Knowing I can care for my husband brings me joy. I know my husband cannot go into a church member's home and see it as a place of refuge and rest — only I can provide that place for him. And though others can sympathize with his crazy schedule, I share those challenges because we live them together. Though this may not always feel like a joy, there is a unique pleasure in sharing in the hardships of ministry. Part of the joy is knowing that our role in serving our husbands is unique. No other person can fill it.

{brian}

Pastors, you need to realize the woman who sleeps alongside you every night and shares your life is the one whom God, in his kind providence, has appointed as your wife and helpmate in your ministry. Encourage your wife to embrace this role. It will contribute not just to her joy in this work but to yours as well.

Second, we have the joy of doing small things that carry great meaning to others in our church. For example, I recently gave one of our older members a ride home from a wedding. I had been asked to take pictures for the couple on their special day. This member had found a way to get to the wedding and wanted to stay for the reception, but she had no way of getting home. Since I planned to be at the reception, I invited her to ride home with me. I really didn't think much about it; it was no great sacrifice on my part. Yet the next day at church, she shared with me how much she had enjoyed being able to spend an hour of time with me. Her comment was, "So many of the young people have your attention on Sunday, and it was nice to be able to just spend that time with you." Her words were a helpful reminder that even in small ways, a pastor's wife can be a blessing to the church. You may not think that sending a card is significant, but because it comes from you, it carries extra weight. The wife of a pastor can have a positive influence on people at church, and noticing them will help them feel encouraged and loved. Doing so doesn't have to involve much work—little touches go a long way!

Third, we have an opportunity to teach our children what it means to care for people in sacrificial ways. Our children are watching how we respond when our husbands are called away, how we respond to criticism, and how we care for hurting and grieving families. They are learning how to visit people in the hospital and how God sustains us in all of these things. Our children are ages six, nine, eleven, and thirteen at present, and they love our church. They love the people in the church, love being at church, and miss our church family when we are away. I am very thankful for this! However, that blessing has not come without some intentional cultivating on our part (more on that later).

Finally, we have a front-row seat to what God is doing. We are able to see firsthand all of the amazing ways God is at work among his people. We experience God's answer to prayers, impart his comfort and wisdom, and are used by God as his instruments. If those realities aren't something to be joyful about, I don't know what is. Ministry life is not easy, but it isn't always a sacrifice and a burden. We must remember the joys and the blessings, especially when we face the challenges and difficulties.

I close with a reminder and an encouragement. Remember that God did not place you in this position accidentally. He has chosen you to be at your current church, with your husband, doing the things you are doing. Know that you are exactly where God wants you to be, whether or not you feel qualified today. Embrace this truth. Grow to love it. And trust that God is using you as the wife of a pastor for his purposes and glory.

Discussion Questions

For a Pastor to Ask His Wife

1. In what ways are you most prone to discouragement? Why?
2. Can you identify an area in our church where you would like to serve?
3. How many people do you have praying for you and your ministry? Who is fighting the battle with you?
4. How are you handling our schedule and other demands, and what changes does our family need to make for you to handle them better?
5. What is the greatest joy you have experienced in being a pastor's wife?

chapter 4

caring for your wife

{brian}

On a cold, clear midmorning three days after Christmas, my beautiful bride-to-be stood before me in front of hundreds of our family and close friends. Our wedding ceremony included the classic vows — "until death do us part." Cara and I committed to "have and to hold" each other from that day forward, and to do so "for better, for worse." We committed to one another "for richer, for poorer, in sickness and in health." We committed to love and cherish the other for the rest of our lives. We made many vows to each other before God and before those gathered there with us.

Although my wife meant every word she spoke in her commitment to me on that day, she would later reflect on that day and realize that many of the unique stresses, pressures, and demands of marriage to a pastor were not an explicit part of our vows. On that day, she did not realize she was marrying a future pastor, and she certainly could not have anticipated how her life would change as the result of marrying one. Even women who knowingly marry a pastor still face difficulties they have no idea await them.

In the last chapter, Cara shared how the challenges of ministry often affect the heart and mind of a pastor's wife. These challenges can lead to discouragement, loss of identity, resentment of the church, and paralyzing fears of what others think — to name only a few! A pastor and his wife share a common solution to these pressures and demands — the power of the gospel of Jesus Christ.

Learning from Peter

Because a pastor is an example to the flock (1 Peter 5:3), Peter's instruction to Christian husbands to "be considerate as you live with your wives" (1 Peter 3:7) is also a helpful template for a pastor who seeks to minister the gospel and care for his wife's soul. Consider Peter's words in their wider context:

> Wives, in the same way submit yourselves to your own husbands so that, if any of them do not believe the word, they may be won over without words by the behavior of their wives, when they see the purity and reverence of your lives. Your beauty should not come from outward adornment, such as elaborate hairstyles and the wearing of gold jewelry or fine clothes. Rather, it should be that of your inner self, the unfading beauty of a gentle and quiet spirit, which is of great worth in God's sight. For this is the way the holy women of the past who put their hope in God used to adorn themselves. They submitted themselves to their own

> husbands, like Sarah, who obeyed Abraham and called him her lord. You are her daughters if you do what is right and do not give way to fear.
>
> Husbands, in the same way be considerate as you live with your wives, and treat them with respect as the weaker partner and as heirs with you of the gracious gift of life, so that nothing will hinder your prayers.
>
> *1 Peter 3:1 – 7*

After Peter instructs Christian wives in the first six verses, he turns to Christian husbands. This passage specifically identifies three reasons that a pastor should minister the gospel and be considerate with his wife.

1. She is a woman of godly character. First, pastors should be gracious and caring toward their wives because of their godly character and behavior (1 Peter 3:1 – 2). Peter wants husbands (and pastors) to realize that even in the difficult times of ministry when a wife struggles, she possesses godly qualities worthy of your appreciation. Take notice of these. The character of a godly wife who is seeking God in the midst of her struggles is a beautiful sight to behold. My wife regularly battles depression and recently went through an especially dark time. The Lord was kind to us through that time, but she was not always herself. Peter's instruction to me to "be considerate" as I live with her took on a whole new meaning. God helped me see that in the midst of her struggles, she continued to care for me and love me. I saw her concern for me and for my ministry. I saw the efforts she made to serve our family. I saw in her heart and in her life the beauty of a gentle, quiet, godly spirit (verse 4) that is precious in the sight of God. Even in my wife's struggle, I found many things to adore about her godly character. In fact, some of these were magnified to me through the difficulties she faced.

2. She is a weaker partner. A pastor should also be considerate with his wife because, as Peter says, she is "the weaker partner." Peter writes that every wife is in some sense a weaker partner because she is a woman (1 Peter 3:7). By this, Peter does not mean that women are somehow inferior to men. He is simply acknowledging that God has made men and women differently, and that one of those differences is that, generally speaking, men are physically stronger than women. Thus, women stand in need of protection and care and should be honored as such. One of the tasks of a husband is to protect his wife from physical harm. Practically, a husband honors his wife as a weaker partner by offering her his help and protection in physical, emotional, and spiritual ways. This can include opening doors for her and helping carry in heavy things from the car, but it can also involve intervening if something dangerous attacks her or threatens her. *(Cara: And ladies, we need to allow our husbands to care for us in this way. It is neither helpful nor encouraging to our husbands if we are always doing these things for ourselves, even if we can. We need to encourage them in their efforts to care for us, both great and small.)*

As mentioned earlier, the pressures and demands of ministry can often be self-imposed, based on expectations that our wife senses from us. When a pastor's wife feels the pressure to be all things for all people in the church, one of the best ways for her husband to protect her is to advise her to say no, giving her permission to be herself and to resist the demands of others. I know that when I help my wife by telling her to say no to requests the church makes of her, she experiences a huge sense of relief. Husbands need to consider what their wives can handle and what they can't, talking this over with them and then seeking to protect their time, emotions, and energy accordingly.

3. She is a sister in Christ. Finally, Peter reminds us that our wives are not just our wives and the mothers of our children; they are also our sisters in Christ. You should treat her as you would a sister in Christ. Quite possibly, Peter was dealing with some husbands who were either physically abusing their wives or were more honoring and respectful to their sisters in Christ in the church than to their own wives. As a pastor, you must guard against treating women in your church better than you would treat your wife, the woman with whom you share your life. Your wife, as a Christian, is "a fellow heir of the grace of life" (1 Peter 3:7 NASB) and shares in the same salvation you do. She is your equal in the sight of God and deserves to be treated with the same grace God has shown to you.

Putting It into Practice

There are at least four practical ways a pastor can show consideration to his wife through the struggles of ministry: by serving her, encouraging her, discipling her, and praying for her. Many of these are natural aspects of pastoral ministry, things a pastor would offer to any member of his congregation, but your wife will need them in a special way from you as her husband.

Serving Your Wife

The great Princeton theologian B. B. Warfield is remembered as one of the toughest, boldest, and most biblically faithful American theologians of the late nineteenth century. His steely glare, seen in most pictures taken of him, would send liberal theologians scampering for cover. Though his appearance can be quite intimidating, it may surprise you to learn of Warfield's legendary example of joyful, sacrificial service to his ailing wife. In his account of the history of Princeton Seminary, David Calhoun vividly captures Warfield's faithful love for his wife:

> Through all the years of their married life Dr. Warfield faithfully cared for his invalid wife. He guarded, protected, and stood by her while carrying his full teaching load and pursuing demanding writing assignments. The seminary students often noted his gentle and loving care for Mrs. Warfield as they walked together on Princeton streets and, later, back and forth on the porch of their campus home. Finally she was bedridden and saw few people besides her husband. By his own choice, Dr. Warfield became almost confined to his house; he was never away from her for more than an hour or two at a time. He set aside time to read to her every day. They left Princeton only once in the ten years before her death, for a vacation that he hoped would help her. With his excellent health and varied interests Dr. Warfield must have felt this restriction, but he never complained.[1]

Warfield spent years constantly caring for his wife, yet J. Gresham Machen once wrote that he believed Warfield had done "about as much work as ten ordinary men" over the course of his lifetime.[2] We can certainly learn from Warfield in the area of theology, but he is also one of those rare men of history whose life example puts our weak excuses for marital neglect to shame. His faithful example of service challenges us to serve our own wives with consistency and longevity.

As a pastor, serving your wife is much the same as it would be for any Christian husband — helping to put the kids to bed, cleaning up the kitchen after dinner, running to the store for milk, and giving her time out by herself. The specific acts of service will vary from marriage to marriage, but there is one simple way of learning how to serve your wife: ask her. Profound, isn't it? Take some time to sit down with her and ask, "What would be the most helpful ways for me to serve you?"

Since circumstances regularly change in ministry and marriage, this question is most effective and helpful when it is asked regularly. A husband may find that serving his wife in one season of life together means helping her to say no to demands on her time because she is overcommitted and doesn't have the time to give. In a different season of life, she may need encouragement to pursue a ministry or interest. As a pastor, serving your wife will vary from day to day and week to week. For example, we can serve our wives by choosing not to have three families over for lunch next Sunday since we already have a busy weekend planned. The key is to be wise and discerning and most of all to communicate with one another.

Encouraging Your Wife

Unfortunately, most men I know stink at encouraging their wives, and pastors are no exception to this trend. Even those who are naturally gifted at encouraging others often fail to practice this in their marriage. It is easy to take for granted the ones we are called to love and value the most — our wives. Pastor and preacher Charles Spurgeon, who was known for his time-consuming preoccupation with his ministry, was still mindful to encourage his wife. We see this illustrated in this story recorded by his wife:

> My beloved husband, always so fully engaged about his Master's business, yet managed to secure many precious moments by

my side, when he would tell me how the work of the Lord was prospering in his hands, and we would exchange sympathies, he comforting me in my suffering, and I cheering him on in his labour.

One ever-recurring question when he had to leave me was, "What can I bring you, wifey?" I seldom answered him by a *request*, for I had all things richly to enjoy, except *health*. But, one day, when he put the usual query, I said, playfully, *"I should like an opal ring, and a piping bullfinch!"* He looked surprised, and rather amused; but simply replied, "Ah, you know I cannot get those for you!" Two or three days we made merry over my singular choice of desirable articles; but, one Thursday evening, on his return from the Tabernacle, he came into my room with such a beaming face, and such love-lighted eyes, that I knew something had delighted him very much. In his hand he held a tiny box, and I am sure his pleasure exceeded mine as he took from it a beautiful little ring, and placed it on my finger. "There is your opal ring, my darling," he said, and then he told me of the strange way in which it had come.[3]

You don't necessarily have to bring home an opal ring to your wife to encourage her, yet when you listen attentively to your wife's desires and go the extra mile to cherish her, you will encourage her and communicate that she is valued and loved. Spurgeon gives a helpful template for doing this. He reminds us that we encourage our wives when we do and say things that make them feel honored and cherished. This is especially true of the wife of a pastor, since your wife will often see you putting in extra, sacrificial effort for the people in your church. Surprise her and take her on a date. Put the same level of sacrificial time and energy you would give to a difficult counseling situation or challenging crisis into showing your wife that she matters to you. I once asked a seasoned pastor of fifty years — a pastor of a very large church — what he did to encourage his wife. He said, "I give my wife a special Christmas present every year: a calendar for the next year that has two date nights a month already scheduled on it." Like this pastor I've found that regular, planned dates really encourage my wife too. As you plan a date, consider the places and activities that she loves, not just what you like to do. Go to where she loves to eat. Do the things she loves to do. At different times throughout the night tell her how grateful you are for all she does to care for you, your family, and your ministry. Write notes and leave them for her — and while you're at it, once in a while leave flowers alongside the notes. Bestow these gestures on her when she is least expecting them. In your notes, mention the things you think she does really well. Write about her godly qualities, and as you do, follow Solomon's example as he instructed his son (Proverbs 5) and Spurgeon's as he served his wife — show your delight in her. *(Cara: Ladies, learn to accept these encouragements. Don't be quick to dismiss them as inauthentic or untrue. Learn to gratefully accept your husband's best efforts to care for and encourage you.)*

If you're struggling in your marriage right now and can't think of a single thing you love about your wife, think back over the years. I can guarantee there was a time when you adored and admired your wife, a time when you vowed before your family and friends to spend your life with her. She may not have said "I do" to the life of ministry, but she spoke those same vows to you. As pastors, we encourage our wives by living with them in a way consistent with God's will for marriage, by studying and knowing them so well that we can encourage them in the areas in which they feel most like a failure. Like a faithful pastor, we pay attention to them, observing and sharing the evidences of God's grace that we see in them.

Discipling Your Wife

Pastors are called to equip and disciple others. As shepherds, we are responsible to teach, mentor, encourage, exhort, rebuke, and lead the people in our church to grow in godliness, grace, and understanding of the truth of God's Word. But pastors are also called to be the principal disciplers of their wives. We love our wives most faithfully when we embrace this role in our families. A pastor should not neglect the importance of caring for the people in his church, but he should be equally concerned for the spiritual care and nurture of his wife and children. This task of discipleship is his responsibility as a husband and father, and it is rooted in the call to leadership the husband must bring to the home.

As a husband and a pastor, you must live with your wife with patience and graciousness, especially when she reveals herself to be the sinner she is. Lovingly shepherd her through her struggles. The unrealistic expectations our churches place on our wives are often the same expectations *we* unknowingly place on them as well. We grow frustrated when they struggle. We forget that they are sinful women who need reminders of the gospel, who forget the truth, who need daily encouragement from us and from the Scriptures. A pastor will tend to live with his wife in a more understanding way when he learns to see her as God sees her — as a sinner saved only by the grace of God.

The specifics of how a pastor disciples his wife can vary, especially if she is a more mature Christian than her husband. In light of this, I asked a few faithful pastors, both young and old, to share some of the practical ways they employ in discipling their wives:

- spend consistent time reading Scripture and praying together
- provide weekly times for her to go out and tend to her own soul
- include her in family worship
- ask her what she found encouraging about being at church on Sunday
- plan a date night in which the conversation focuses on her
- regularly ask her what has been encouraging and discouraging in her life
- buy books for her you think might be helpful for her to read
- offer feedback on a teaching she has watched or listened to and discuss it together
- take her to a conference with you
- send her blog posts and articles that will encourage her

Don't lose sight of the many ways *you* will grow in your own walk with Christ as you make these intentional efforts to spiritually care for your bride. The wonderful blessing of marriage is that if your wife is growing spiritually, it will encourage *you* in your own growth.

Praying for Your Wife

Many husbands struggle to pray *for* their wives *with* their wives. You may be surprised, however, to know that many *pastors* have trouble praying for their wives *with* their wives. You may be asking why this is. My best guess is that this act does not come naturally for most men. Yet this simple act — praying for your wife in her presence —

could be the best way to help your wife feel loved by you. Start by praying for your wife when you are alone and then calling her or sending a text or an e-mail telling her you did. When you pray for her, pray for the things you are learning about her and her needs as you spiritually care for her and encourage her.

A simple method to learn what to pray for is to sit down with her when you are alone, look her in the eyes, and ask her how you can pray for her. Then pray with her about those things. It's that simple. Pastors, own your failure in this area if you have neglected praying with your wife. Confess the hypocrisy of fervently praying with others in your church but failing to do so with your wife. If you haven't been loving, leading, protecting, and caring for your wife well, she is apt to receive that renewed effort positively. If she is a godly woman, it is likely that she has been praying for you and asking God to do this very work in you! Your actions could be the answers to her prayers.

I love and adore my wife for many, many reasons, but one of them is the way she prayed for me early in our marriage. At the time, I was already serving in ministry but wasn't leading my wife or doing many of the things I suggest in this book. I was not living with her in a way that showed I understood God's will for me as a husband. To her credit, she didn't complain or nag me about this. Instead, she prayed for me. It took about two years, but eventually, new to ministry and marriage, I came to a breaking point and realized I didn't know God's Word well. My wife recognized that this was missing in my life and at my request began to teach me how to study my Bible.

The Lord did a miraculous, awakening work in me almost overnight, and I began to devour God's Word for hours each night. Years later, I learned that my wife had been consistently praying that God would one day give me a great love for his Word. I truly believe I am a pastor today because God did that work in me in response to my wife's faithful prayers. She didn't accomplish this through guilt trips, nagging, or threats, but with a gentle, quiet spirit that is precious in the sight of God. God answered the prayers of a godly woman.

As a pastor and husband, I know that your wife has at least one thing in common with mine: she is a sinner saved by the grace of God, who struggles through life's difficulties and is often overwhelmed by the demands of your ministry. Your wife needs and deserves your most patient, gracious, and enduring care. Being a pastor's wife is a tough role — one that most women don't expect to fill on their wedding day. We can help make that burden a joy, turning the demands of ministry into opportunities to serve others, transforming the pressures and tensions of being a pastor's wife into a sanctifying influence in her life. It all begins with prayer, bringing the challenges, needs, struggles, and joys of our wives before the Lord and learning to love, nurture, cherish, and honor them through it all.

Discussion Questions

For a Pastor to Ask His Wife

1. What are the most helpful ways I can serve you?
2. What things do I do, or can I do, that encourage you most?
3. In what ways can I disciple you better and pray for you more intentionally and faithfully?
4. What stands in your way of receiving my care? Are there any barriers or obstacles that we need to remove?
5. How can you help me do a better job of caring for you?

Reflection

Keeping Your Marriage Strong

Cathi Johnson

My husband, Bob, and I were married in 1983. When we began our marriage, Bob was serving in full-time ministry, and after six years he accepted a position as a senior pastor. At the time, he was twenty-nine years old. He had just begun working on his Master of Divinity degree, and I was pregnant with our second child.

The grace, goodness, and protection of the Lord were upon us during this time. We tried our best to balance the needs of the church with the care of our own marriage and our growing family. My own learning curve involved laying down my selfish ambitions, getting myself out of the way of what God wanted to do in my life. I was just beginning to understand that my life was not really about me and my comforts — it was a calling from God to support my husband in his call to ministry, a call to love him and be his helpmate. My self-centeredness was continually colliding (and still does) with the selflessness that is needed to be a pastor's wife.

After more than a quarter century of marriage and ministry together, we've been taught by the Lord that it is vitally important to daily depend on his Spirit and that I can faithfully and obediently love the Lord by loving my husband and loving the church he has been called to pastor and lead. As a pastor's wife, I've sought several ways to keep our marriage strong.

1. I realized that security in my marriage provides security for our church. *Purpose to love and enjoy each other* as a gift to your flock.

2. Bob and I have found it helpful to *establish shared goals together.* This helps me avoid feeling like I am competing for his time and attention with the church. Through our shared ministry goals we partner together to serve others.

3. I've found it helpful to *remember that God has given me as a gift to my husband.* Your husband needs what you have to offer him. God will work through your words, your touch, and your acts of service to bless and encourage your husband in his calling. Encourage his confidence and be a good listener. Don't be afraid to speak honestly to him, but avoid harsh judgments and critical words. It's not your responsibility to fix him.

4. *Be wise and discerning in your relationships with other women* in your church and in the community. Be careful what you share when you are "out with the girls" and among friends. Pray for sensitivity and wisdom when you are talking about your husband and others in the church, for Satan can easily gain a place in your heart if you give in to the toxic sin of gossip.

5. *Keep the lines of communication open* with your husband. Communication is the lifeblood of your relationship. Don't ignore that feeling of being distant from your husband. Paul tells us to address problems and conflicts when they arise so that we keep the Devil from gaining a foothold (Ephesians 4:26–27). When you are hurt by your husband, pray for grace and for the ability to see his side of the conflict. Pray for humility to express yourself to him without accusing him of intentions he may not have.

6. *Plan a weekly time to share your schedules.* This helps each of you value what you are uniquely called to do in your life together. Sharing your schedules also ensures a measure of accountability and helps you avoid unexpected surprises.

7. *Make your home and marriage a place of joy* for your husband. Work to make your husband intoxicated with you, staying attractive to him so that he has no reason to look outside your marriage for comfort. Develop your home into a sanctuary of peace and acceptance for him. Build a sense of belonging to one another by planning traditions and sharing favorite activities together. Schedule blocks of time when you can relax, have fun, and laugh together. Learn together by sharing from books and articles you are reading and how you are being challenged from Scripture. Ask each other good questions.

Dream together. Set future goals. This kind of camaraderie creates hope and excitement in your marriage.

A unique and special joy comes from serving the Lord together in ministry. Protect that joy. His church is worth it.

Cathi Johnson is a pastor's wife who has served alongside her husband, Bob, for over thirty years.

part 3

the pastor's children

"Daddy, Can't You Stay Home Tonight?"

chapter 5

shepherding individually

{brian}

The notion of shepherding one's own children individually is a foreign concept to many Christians, including pastors. It was new to me when I first heard of it. For many years, I labored to spend time caring for individual church members while completely disregarding the need to pastor my own children. That changed when I was challenged to take up this task by a rather unlikely person. It was not a fellow pastor. Neither was it a conference speaker or author or some other "expert" on the subject. It was a man who serves as a deacon at his church. He's a pharmacist, married with seven children. The faithful example of this man completely changed my understanding of what it meant for a man to shepherd his family.

Every pastor needs to take seriously his responsibility to disciple personally each one of his children individually. The task of shepherding your children falls into the mix of other demands in life. When children are neglected, feelings of resentment and bitterness can develop in their hearts. They may begin to resent people in the church and may even transfer some of that resentment to God. Pastors face many demands on their time, but it is important for them to prioritize the spiritual growth and development of their own children, modeling to other fathers an obedience to the commands of Deuteronomy 6:4 – 9 and Ephesians 6:4. Sometimes it's hard to know what this looks like. This chapter will help you cultivate patterns in your weekly schedule to shepherd each of your children, helping you to spend that time well.

Shepherding Your Children

Like most pastors, you probably affirm the importance of shepherding the souls of your children. But the real issue isn't whether or not you affirm it; it's "Do you have a plan?" Many pastors believe it's important to disciple their own children, but they lack a deliberate and practical plan to accomplish it. They may have developed effective and deliberate discipleship structures in their local church ministry, but for some reason they cannot do so in their own home. I suggest five simple ways a pastor can begin to establish in his household these deliberate structures that will help him to care spiritually for his children.

1. Shepherd individually. Some great resources are available for developing habits of engaging in family worship, and many Christian families are experiencing renewal in this area (more on that in the next chapter). But the single most significant task you'll face as a father is not leading family worship; it's meeting one-on-one with each of your children to read God's Word, engage their hearts, and pray together. I am convinced that this practice forms the foundation for the individual spiritual care of each child. The deacon I mentioned earlier who was an example in discipling his seven children was intentional in this regard. With seven children and seven days in each week, he established a schedule that allowed him to meet with each child one day a week. He met with them in the morning to read and pray together. Since Cara and I had just over half the number of children he did (and still do), I could hardly argue that I didn't have enough time. His example not only inspired me; it left me without any excuses.

I started meeting with each of our children Monday through Thursday. I reserved a night for each child. When it was their night to be with Dad, the child stayed up thirty minutes later than usual, and we read Scripture, prayed, and picked out a fun book to read alone with me. Our times together would often end in a wrestling match. Initially, I thought my children would lose interest after a few weeks — but I was wrong. The children are actually my greatest source of accountability in this area, and they remember when it is their night. This weekly time with them has blessed me as a father, but it would never have gotten started if I hadn't been intentional and made it a priority. *(Cara: Wives, do you know what this means for you? You'll have to be willing to sacrifice some of your time with your husband to ensure that his time with the kids happens. I don't give this time to them jealously; I see it as a sacrifice I make for the welfare of my children and their growth in Christ.)*

Make sure you are instructing and interacting with your child in some way — just the two of you — and you will begin to see with greater depth into their lives and hearts. You will learn things about them that you never knew. Just as my friend challenged me, I now give you this challenge. If you do not have a regular pattern of meeting individually with each of your children, start this week! As a pastor, you will instruct and individually meet with many of your church members this week. Make sure you are showing the same love and care to your own children.

2. Shepherd biblically. Instruct and discipline your children, using God's Word. I realize this may seem fairly obvious to a pastor, but I've seen pastors who spend more time focused on teaching principles from the catechism and from God's Word than on reading the Bible itself. It's possible to go through several rounds of discipline and teaching and yet never reference what God actually says about the behavior in question. And while biblical principles are good and helpful, make sure you are also teaching your children to know and memorize actual Bible verses.

Pastors have a unique opportunity in this regard. You can prepare your children for Sunday worship each week by using the passage you are preparing to preach on, teaching them what you are learning. When I meet individually with each of our children, I read with them the passage I am going to preach on the next Sunday. This practice allows me to shepherd their souls with God's Word and has the advantage of preparing them to hear the message for the upcoming Sunday. Working through this passage with them, I'm able to see and address areas that might be hard for them to understand and also equip them to better hear and respond to the Word of God when it is preached in our corporate gathering. Regardless of the passage you choose, make sure your instruction and discipline are biblical — that you are using God's Word in such a way that your child knows that what you teach comes from God himself.

3. Shepherd theologically. Adults notoriously underestimate the ability of children to understand deep theological truths about God and the gospel, and pastors are just as guilty of doing this as anyone. Children can and should learn theological truth, even at a young age. Obviously, we need to instruct them at a level that matches their ability to understand. But don't assume that children can't learn and remember theological truth. One of our church members recently told me that he had overheard his eight-year-old teaching his four-year-old about the Trinity, and his explanation was clear, understandable, and appropriate for his age.

None of us would disagree that it is important to teach our kids about the gospel, particularly, the fact that Jesus died for our sins. However, have you dared to teach concepts like imputation (the great exchange in which Christ bore our sins on the cross in our place and Christ gave us his perfect righteousness instead)? I have personally watched four- and five-year-old children grasp this great, essential theological truth of the gospel. If children are able to understand, we should instruct them in this truth. Children are also good at grasping the broad themes of redemptive history. Consider the things you teach regularly to adults, and don't be afraid to teach these same truths to your children. Be clear and simple, but don't water down or leave out difficult topics. The act of teaching truth to children may even improve your teaching of adults by forcing you to focus on the essential message you want to communicate.

4. Shepherd prayerfully. Part of our individual instruction for our children in the Lord has to do with how to approach God in prayer. We should pray *for* our children. We should pray *with* our children. We should pray for wisdom as we instruct our children. We should pray with our children after we discipline them. We should pray for our children with the whole family. We should pray for others with our children. Pastors have a privileged knowledge of the specific needs of church members and should be praying for the church with their children. As we consistently pray in these ways, we instruct our children about how to pray and model what a life of prayer — what Paul calls "pray[ing] without ceasing" (1 Thessalonians 5:17 NASB) — looks like. As you prayerfully instruct them, make sure you are instructing them about being able to go to God in prayer, telling them of the gracious work of our great high priest and mediator, Jesus Christ. Teach them that Jesus is at the right hand of the Father, interceding on our behalf every time we pray (Hebrews 4:14 – 16; 9:24). Our prayers are heard by God because of what Jesus has done for us.

{cara}

A practical way to encourage this kind of daily prayer is through a prayer calendar. Brian set up a church directory so members of our church can pray for each member in a single month. A friend of mine had the brilliant idea of putting these names on index cards attached together. Each day, we flip a card over to see which person we are to pray for on that day. The index cards sit on our kitchen table to remind us to pray for the people at mealtimes. This routine has encouraged the habit of praying for our church members and remembering their needs daily.

5. *Shepherd sacrificially.* Pastors are busy, and they face many demands on their time. My wife and I wrote this book because we understand the challenges pastors face. We know how difficult it is to maintain a healthy balance between the needs of ministry and the call to be faithful to our families. There is no easy road to success. The weekly, individual care of your children will not happen without sacrifice. You will have to sacrifice some extra sleep in the morning or some downtime in the evening. You may miss your favorite television show or sports event; you may have to give up the time to read that book you're looking forward to digesting. Prepare yourself, as you commit to this, to lose some of your current "benefits." Still, the sacrifice in this short season of life when your children are living in your home is well worth the loss of time. Not only that, but the task of shepherding your children is a key part of your calling as a pastor (1 Timothy 3:4 – 5) and can even be the means the Lord uses to help your family grow deeper in their love for God and his church instead of becoming disenchanted and bitter.

Fostering Appreciation

Many pastors and their congregations assume a pastor's children will somehow naturally grow to love the gospel, the ministry, and the church. This is a naive assumption. Children will not naturally grow to love the ministry, nor are they guaranteed to love and value the local church in which their father serves. As pastors, we must intentionally teach the gospel to our children and work to foster an appreciation of the local church and our calling to serve the church. We should do this in a spirit of prayer, depending on the Holy Spirit to work in their hearts.

I have found five principles that are useful in teaching children about the work of pastoral ministry. Understanding these principles helps each child grasp what a pastor does and why it is important work.

In teaching this, I seek to cultivate love for pastoral ministry rather than resentment for the time their father spends away from home.

1. "My work is very important to God." Through the writings of the apostle Paul, God teaches that the work of the pastor is good and necessary work (1 Timothy 3:1). It is work that keeps us on the edge of life and death, the temporal and the eternal. The local church is the primary vehicle through which God chooses to usher in his coming kingdom in the world, and the work of a pastor is unlike any other labor. Pastors must first understand this themselves. They must value the work of ministry before they can teach this value to their own children. A pastor needs to help his children realize that when their dad is working and away from home at different times, he is not goofing off or wasting time. He does not leave the home because he wants to be away from them. When their father is away, children need to know that the work he is doing is kingdom-building work that serves Christ in a special way.

Whenever the opportunity arises, pastors should include their children in the work they do. There are appropriate times when kids can accompany them on hospital and home visits, help them set up for church activities, pray for church members at the dinner table, and even contribute to their sermon preparation. There is great benefit for both the family and congregation when their children are involved in this way. So be sure to make the extra effort to plan and intentionally include your children. At the very least, it will help them appreciate the important work their dad is doing.

{cara}

We also need to emphasize that the work Daddy is leaving us to do is very important to God as well. Instead of being envious of our hus-

bands' lunches out or even their golf outings, we need to remind our children (and at times ourselves) that our husbands are building relationships and meeting needs. We need to joyfully ask our husbands about their time and conversations at our next family gathering so we can celebrate the work God has been doing while they have been away. We can also accomplish this by praying with our children for our husbands when they're away from home.

2. *"God's Word is how God changes people."* A common question from pastors' children, especially if a pastor has an office at home, is "Daddy, why do you study so much?" I once had a pastor with young kids ask me, "How do you respond to the child who comes to your office door at home and asks, 'Daddy, are you still working?' " You should carefully answer that question in a way that teaches them to value what you do instead of just trying to get them to leave you alone for a few more minutes. Help them to understand that only God's Word through the power of the Holy Spirit changes people, awakening them and bringing them from death to life. Teach them that God has entrusted their dad with a great responsibility to teach and preach God's Word to God's people so they can know God better and become more like Jesus. This demands that a pastor is faithful and diligent to present himself as "a worker who does not need to be ashamed and who correctly handles the word of truth" (2 Timothy 2:15). Avoid speaking poorly of your work or communicating to your children that what you do is a hardship or burden. Speak positively of the power and responsibility of handling God's Word well.

3. *"I need to have a 'talk' with someone."* We've often used this phrase with our children when I am meeting someone for discipleship, returning the phone call of an upset church member, addressing a disastrous consequence as the result of someone's sin, or persuading an angry wife not to walk out on her husband. My children do not need to know the details of these situations, and if they were to learn them, it could even harm them. When I need to spend time helping someone or talking on the phone, I try to help my children realize that God has gifted their daddy with the ability to talk with people about their problems, share God's Word with them, and encourage them to follow Jesus more faithfully. Teach children why you need to talk with people, but don't go into details or try to explain every situation.

4. "It is a joy to serve and care for God's people." Most people in the world spend their days laboring to provide for their families by working at a business, dealing with customers, or meeting the needs of people through some form of service. Pastors have the privilege of spending most of their time studying God's Word and caring for God's people. What a special honor pastors have been given by God! Communicate that honor to your children. Even when faced with difficulty in your ministry, teach your children about the untainted joy of your work. Serving and caring for God's people *is* a joy. Of course, if the work is not joyful for you, effectively communicating this to children will be difficult, if not impossible. A pastor or pastor's wife who is disenchanted about the work of ministry will inevitably raise children who become disenchanted with ministry and the church.

{cara}

Brian's word of caution bears repeating. We must be careful as we are discussing church matters that we do not burden our children with unnecessary details about church life. In an effort to teach them to love the church, we need to remember that carrying the burdens of the church is not their job. One of our children is highly perceptive of people's feelings and attitudes. She can often tell when something is wrong with someone or a family. Because of this ability, she can decipher pieces of our conversations (when we don't even realize she is listening) and become burdened for the family. We have to be cautious because she is not mature enough to know how to handle those burdens. We need to remember that our children are listening, whether or not we realize it, and therefore we need to be careful as we talk about our ministry. A good rule of thumb is to have hard conversations deliberately away from the children.

We do not hide everything from our children. They need to develop an awareness that we live in a fallen world that is filled with sin. We have conversations with our children about divorce, death, and suicide. However, we have these conversations in the context of biblical truths that help us better understand God's plan for his people.

5. "These people keep asking about you." Regardless of where and how God has called you as a pastor, there is always someone who will love you and your family and will want to care for you. This is especially true as you serve in the same local church for many years. Remember these people, the ones who ask you about your family. Tell your children about them. Let your kids know they are loved by people in the church, people whom their father cares for. Some of my sweetest relationships in my church are with people who care for my wife and our children. I think of a ninety-year-old widow who dearly loves our oldest daughter (arguably more than she loves me, her pastor). They have a special relationship that is a joy to see.

Remind your children that the people of your church love them, ask about them, and appreciate the sacrifice they make to allow their dad to serve the church.

The value of encouraging our children in this regard was affirmed after preaching at an out-of-town marriage conference. One of the elders from that church handwrote our four children a three-page letter, which they received in the mail about a week after my return. The content of this letter encouraged our kids, and it was encouraging to my wife and me as well.

> Thank you for sharing your parents with our church family just a few days ago! I think you will be happy to know that God used them to encourage people to love the Lord more, trust his Word, and live by faith ... To say thank you for your part in our 2012 family conference, get a treat at Dairy Queen. I hope you like ice cream ... You all did play a part in our conference, and I appreciate it! Every time you give your blessing to the ministry opportunities God gives your parents, you are involved in their work.

This elder listed several ways our children could bless and support our ministry—praying for us, being thankful for us, speaking honestly with us, and so on. Attached to the letter was a $25 gift card to Dairy Queen. This letter illustrates how people can help a pastor's children realize the important role they play as children of a pastor. With God's help, this encouragement will help them grow to love and appreciate the ministry their father does, not resent it.

Pastors have that same responsibility to their own children. This task is best accomplished when we make an investment in shepherding the souls of each of them, spend deliberate time with them, and help them understand the honor, not burden, of watching and participating in their daddy's important work. And yet, this task of shepherding the family is not accomplished solely in individual discipleship and instruction, but also when the pastor shepherds the souls of his entire family *together.*

Discussion Questions

For a Wife to Ask Her Husband

1. Do you meet at a consistent, sustainable interval with each of our children? ***If not:*** Why not? How can we arrange our schedule so you have time available to do so? How often does each child need to have time with you? Is a weekly meeting too often, or not often enough? ***If so:*** How do you determine the way you will spend that time?
2. How do we foster a love for your work in our children?
3. Have you lost your joy in carrying out the work of ministry? If so, what can you do to regain it?

chapter 6

shepherding together

{brian}

Charles Spurgeon was a mighty man of God — an effective evangelist and pastor. Many different people in his life helped shape him into the man he became, but one person often overlooked and underestimated in her influence is Spurgeon's mother. Spurgeon recounts some impactful moments when his mother gathered her children around the dinner table:

> It was the custom, on Sunday evenings, while we were yet little children, for her to stay at home with us, and then we sat round the table, and read verse by verse, and she explained the Scripture to us. After that was done, then came the time of pleading; there was a little piece of Alleine's Alarm, or of Baxter's Call to the Unconverted, and this was read with pointed observations

> made to each of us as we sat round the table; and the question was asked, how long it would be before we would think about our state, how long before we would seek the Lord. Then came a mother's prayer, and some of the words of that prayer we shall never forget, even when our hair is grey. I remember, on one occasion, her praying thus: "Now Lord, if my children go on in their sins, it will not be from ignorance that they perish, and my soul must bear a swift witness against them at the day of judgment if they lay not hold of Christ." That thought of a mother's bearing swift witness against me, pierced my conscience, and stirred my heart.[1]

Spurgeon's memories of his mother remind us of the significant role godly mothers play in shepherding the souls of their children and also show us that God works in distinctive ways when families are instructed together.

Although mothers play an essential role in the instruction of their children, Scripture tells us that God has called the father, as head of the family, to take the lead in this area. Douglas Kelly writes, "The representative principle inherent in God's covenant dealings with our race indicates that the head of each family is to represent his family before God in divine worship and that the spiritual atmosphere and long-term personal welfare of that family will be affected in large measure by the fidelity — or failure — of the family head in this area."[2]

Pastors should be intentional about ministering to their children individually, as we urged in the last chapter, but it is also important that he shepherd his family in some form of family worship. And pastors have a special opportunity to prepare their families for corporate worship gatherings with the rest of the church family as well.

No clear, biblical text requires a father to lead family worship, yet there are many passages with commands that strongly imply the need for corporate instruction in the home. Paul's instruction to the family in Colossians 3:18–21 is a good example, as is this instruction in his letter to the Ephesians:

> Children, obey your parents in the Lord, for this is right. "Honor your father and mother" — which is the first commandment with a promise — "so that it may go well with you and that you may enjoy long life on the earth."
>
> Fathers, do not exasperate your children; instead, bring them up in the training and instruction of the Lord.
>
> *Ephesians 6:1 – 4*

In his instruction to both the Colossian and Ephesian churches, Paul gives three basic principles that underlie the need for regular family worship under the leadership of the father.

1. Families publicly worshiped together. We know that many of the New Testament letters from Paul (like Colossians and Ephesians) were addressed to several different churches and were read aloud in their entirety to the gathered church body.

Each member of the family is addressed — wives (Colossians 3:18), husbands (Colossians 3:19), children (Colossians 3:20; Ephesians 6:1), fathers (Colossians 3:21; Ephesians 6:4), and even slaves (Colossians 3:22). From this we can conclude that Paul assumed that all of these people would be gathered to hear his letter read and would benefit from his instructions. Paul wrote his letters knowing that children would be there with their parents, husbands would be present with their wives. Each group would be able to hear the instruction that Paul was directing to the other groups present.

Spouses would know what God expected from the other spouse. Children would know how God expected their parents to act toward them as well as toward one another (as husband and wife) in their marriage.

2. Parents instructed their children in the home. Colossians does not directly mention this instruction to Christian fathers (3:21), but Paul's letter to the Ephesians clearly states that fathers (and likely mothers as well) should not exasperate or provoke their children to anger but should instruct and discipline them in the Lord (6:4). Deuteronomy 6 illustrates this idea in practical ways, showing how fathers were to teach their children the truth about God, God's desire for their complete devotion, and the need to discuss and study God's Word in the home. It is likely that Paul intended Christian parents to obey Ephesians 6:4 by following the pattern of Deuteronomy 6 — providing instruction about God, his expectations, and his Word in the home. Like the families of Israel, a Christian family should be marked by regular spiritual interaction between parents and children.

{cara}

It doesn't matter if you are a stay-at-home mom or a work-outside-the-home mom; you are responsible to assist in the training that your husband leads. This training doesn't always have to include a formal time when you gather together. Even in our everyday activities we are setting an example for the children of trusting God and thanking him in all situations. We need to show a love for God and his Word and encourage our children to memorize verses and study the Bible with us. By submitting ourselves to our husbands' teaching and leading, we encourage our children to submit to their dads' authority and teaching. As a wife I model this by being just as engaged during our family worship times as I expect my children to be. When my husband is gone, I reinforce what he has taught by continuing to have conversations with my children about the Scripture for the week. I try to model note taking during our Sunday services and encourage our kids to take notes, even if it was in the form of drawing pictures before they learned to write.

3. Children submitted to their parents' teaching. The fiery Reformer and pastor Martin Luther recognized his responsibility to lead his family as a pastor and father. He called the home both a school and a church and compared the role of the father in the home to that of a bishop or a priest: "Abraham had in his tent a house of God and a church, just as today any godly and pious head of a household instructs his children ... in godliness. Therefore such a house is actually a school and a church, and the head of the household is a bishop and priest in his house."[3]

Scripture tells us that parents should instruct and discipline their children. It also tells us that children are to obey their parents (Colossians 3:20; Ephesians 6:1). Paul reminds the children gathered at the church in Colossae that this obedience "pleases the Lord" (3:20). Clearly, Christian fathers in the early church took time to have spiritual conversations about God in their homes and taught their children to be fully devoted to God by following Christ. As parents they modeled for their children what it was like to be a follower of Jesus. The responsibility of the children? Obey what they had been taught, put into practice what they had learned.

Pastors have an wonderful opportunity, not only to lead their own family in worship, but to prepare them for corporate worship in the local church. Here are a few suggestions as you prepare to lead your family in preparation for corporate worship.

Choose the sermon text for the next Sunday as the Scripture reading for your family worship time. When you know the text you will be preaching on for the upcoming Sunday and have some of the ideas worked out for the sermon, share these insights and ideas with your family. Through this practice, I learned that our children were able to listen to the sermon and catch important truths from it at younger ages than I would have thought possible.[4] In addition, do not underestimate the valuable insights, questions, and illustrations your wife and children may contribute. Often, I find that their input at this point in the week makes my sermon stronger, helping our congregation to better understand the truth of God's Word.

Sing a hymn or worship song that is planned for the upcoming Sunday. Most pastors play some role in planning the service, so you will likely know which songs will be included. This habit encourages children who cannot read well to engage in the singing time during corporate worship. Over the years, our hymn singing during family worship has developed a confidence in my children to sing well in both private and public contexts of worship.

Pray for the immediate needs of the congregation. Fathers can choose different ways to lead their families to pray together. Whether you pray for the missionaries of your church or for church members who are sick and suffering, teach your children how to pray for people. Be wise in how much you share, but still give your children (and wife) specific ways to pray.

Preparing your family for public worship is not your chief aim during your family worship time, and you may not do it every time you meet as a family. But it's a great opportunity for helping your children value the experience of worship with the gathered church. It also helps them grasp the continuity between their private worship experience in the home and their public worship with the church. As a pastor, you have a wonderful chance to show your children — and model for your congregation — the essential unity between our private and public worship.

Jonathan Edwards, who is known as one of America's greatest pastors and theologians, modeled this faithfulness well. In addition to the list of his academic and literary accolades, we should add the commendation of "faithful husband and father." One of Edwards's biographers, George Marsden, captures the commitment Edwards had to pastor his own family:

> [Edwards] began the day with private prayers followed by family prayers, by candlelight in winter. Each meal was accompanied by household devotions, and at the end of each day Sarah joined him in his study for prayers ...
>
> Care for his children's souls was, of course, his preeminent concern. In morning devotions he quizzed them on Scripture with questions appropriate to their ages ...[5]

If we read just this short summary, it's easy to miss the significance of these daily acts of teaching, training, and pastoral care. Edwards was faithful in shepherding the souls of his family, which bore fruit in his public roles as a pastor and scholar. The impact of his parenting and his future kingdom fruitfulness are demonstrated in the fact that his eleven children continued to follow the Lord long after he was gone. Edwards had the wisdom and discernment to look to the future and to recognize that — even with all of the important things he had to do as a pastor and church leader — this family shepherding task was important. It was important because his children's souls were at stake. It was important enough that he willingly said no to other ministry demands so he could focus on caring for his family. And it was important enough that even in the midst of a very fruitful ministry, he made time for his children. Sadly, many pastors, even many who were contemporaries of Edwards, were not as faithful in this task of shepherding their families, and it sometimes led to devastating consequences. Edwards's example motivates us to faithfulness, just as the examples of those who were negligent function as a warning. What will be your spiritual legacy as a father and a pastor? In the last chapter, we'll dig into that question as we look at how the things we do today determine the future of our children and our family.

Discussion Questions

For a Pastor and His Wife to Discuss Together

1. Why is it important for a family to worship together?
2. How should we be working together to do this? What are we doing right now that is good? What could we change or do differently?
3. What specific role should a husband have in family worship? What should a wife do? What role do the children have in our family times of worship?
4. How can we use our time of family worship to better teach and prepare our children for our corporate gatherings on Sunday?

chapter 7

shepherding looking forward

{brian}

One of the most celebrated missionaries in the history of the church, David Livingstone, died filled with great regret. Though Livingstone accomplished much in the name of Christ, reaching lost people with the good news of the gospel, Doreen Moore writes of the regret and sorrow that Livingstone carried with him until the day he died. After Livingstone's wife, Mary, died, he was led to reflect on "his shortcomings as a husband and father." He had many regrets and wanted to start over. The sorrows he had put his family through caused him to wonder if he should have just remained celibate.[1]

As we saw in the first chapter, great success in ministry does not always correspond to great success in parenting and marriage. In fact, one of the hardest things for a pastor to do is give higher priority to his time with his wife and children.

One of the most celebrated, perhaps even idolized, ministry figures in the last half century is the evangelist Billy Graham. He is celebrated for good reason. Millions of people all over the world have heard the gospel through his preaching. Hundreds of thousands claim to have been converted under his ministry.[2] Graham's ministry has been a model for other evangelistic efforts, and he remains an iconic figure, especially in the Southern Baptist Convention. If anyone in the world should be able to have some peace, knowing that his life had made a difference in God's kingdom, surely Billy Graham would have that assurance.

In light of his astounding ministry success, it's important for pastors, evangelists, and missionaries who are tempted to forsake their families for the sake of their ministries to hear these sobering words from Billy Graham:

> This is a difficult subject for me to write about, but over the years, the BGEA and the Team became my second family without my realizing it. Ruth [his wife] says those of us who were off traveling missed the best part of our lives — enjoying the children as they grew. She is probably right. I was too busy preaching all over the world.
>
> Only Ruth and the children can tell what those extended times of separation meant to them. For myself, as I look back, I now know that I came through those years much the poorer both psychologically and emotionally. I missed so much by not being home to see the children grow and develop. The children must carry scars of those separations too ...
>
> I now warn young evangelists not to make the mistakes I did.[3]

Graham also writes about the good times he had with his children when he was around. He has spoken about the love he had and still has for them. By God's grace, he has good relationships with his children as he comes to the end of his life. God has truly been gracious and faithful to the Graham family. And though Graham was not guilty of deliberate neglect, he still harbors regrets. As Graham candidly shares, his biggest regret isn't about another place he should have visited or a sermon he would have liked to preach one more time or a desire to have reached more people with the gospel (although I assume even he would have some regrets here). The regret that rises to the forefront of his memories has to do with the way he treated his family, making them a low priority in his life.

Those who carry out pastoral ministry today need to listen to the warnings of men like Graham. We need to learn from the past and listen to the wise words of those who have accomplished great things for God, yet have regrets at the end. We must learn from their mistakes. Be attentive to the warning signs, and be prepared to make the necessary changes to avoid neglectful patterns in your marriage and family. It is not too late to repent and make the life adjustments that will allow you to shepherd faithfully the souls of your family members. With this in mind, I offer four warning signs to look for, signs that may lead to regrets at the end of your ministry if they aren't addressed today.

Four Warning Signs of Neglect

If as you drive your car you come across a caution sign that reads, "Warning: Cliff Ahead. Turn Around Now," you'd be a fool to keep blindly driving ahead. Yet that's exactly what many pastors do. They see the warning signs but do nothing to change the direction their life is heading. As you read through this next section, prayerfully consider if any of these signs are evident in your life. If they are, begin by getting on your knees and crying out to God for help. Then find someone — a trusted older pastor or close friend — to ask to help you make the changes you need to make to repent and get your life back on track.

1. You are in a struggling marriage. A number of married couples recognize they have marital problems, but wrongly assume they will just fix them themselves. Pastors are no different. If anything, pastors face even greater barriers to opening up and being honest. They face strong temptations to hide or cover up their marital difficulties to keep them from the church. A pastor's marriage can be broken for a number of reasons, some related to the relationship itself, others related to the special challenges and pressures of pastoral ministry. Regardless of the cause of the struggle, if your marriage is broken you will need help to put it back together. I would advise you to seek outside help for the sake of your marriage, your children, and your ministry (1 Timothy 3:4 – 5). As I mentioned earlier, your marriage and the way it portrays the gospel and models Christ to others is an essential aspect of your pastoral ministry. If your marriage is struggling, your ministry is struggling — even if everything seems to be fine in the church. Pause to honestly assess the problems in your marriage relationship, and where there are areas of brokenness, take steps to save it. *(Cara: Wives, I cannot stress enough the need to be open, honest, and transparent with our husbands. We have to be proactive in protecting our marriages. We need to be willing to receive correction. We must forgive our husbands* *graciously when they fail us, and we must be quick to apologize and ask for forgiveness when we fail them.)*

2. You are dealing with a bitter child. The cliché of the rebellious, bitter pastor's kid (PK) or missionary's kid (MK) exists for a very good reason — it's often true. Billy Graham once reflected on the life of a PK: "PKs often have difficult, if not disastrous, periods in their lives. Maybe people expect too much of them because of their parentage. Or maybe they themselves expect too much, making unreasonably high demands on themselves in order to live up to others' expectations."[4] In addition to the issue of unrealistic expectations, I'd like to add another reason many PKs struggle. Conversations I've had with PKs and MKs over the years have led me to believe that some of their rebellion against their parents and their disenchantment with the church came from broken promises, promises their parents made over the years and failed to keep.

A pastor may promise his son he will be at a ball game, but he finds he didn't have time to finish his sermon prep and has to keep studying. Or he may promise to be home for dinner at a certain time, but he consistently arrives home late. A pastor may promise his daughter he will read with her tonight, only to find that the phone call with the troubled church member takes longer than expected. When a pastor experiences the pressure of ministry demands, it's not just his wife who suffers from neglect; PKs and MKs experience distinctive pressures as well — and the most common is a pattern of broken promises. This pattern chips away at their dad's credibility. Broken promises translate into hypocrisy, and it is easy for a child to transfer their disillusionment with their father to their faith in God. While a bitter child is ultimately the result of a sinful heart that needs Christ, we'd be foolish to ignore the important influence that a father has in forming his children. If you have a pattern of broken promises with your family, you need to assess the effect this can have on their willingness to trust what you say. The long-term results can be serious.

3. You have a demanding church. All churches make demands on their pastors, but some are more demanding than others. Some have learned how to respect the boundaries set by the pastor for his family; others have not. You will need to take a close look at the way the church treats your family and carefully establish boundaries to protect your time with your loved ones. Part of your assessment will be to determine if the demands are really coming from the church or if they are self-inflicted. Over the years, the types of demands and the expectations of the church I am serving have changed. When I first came to the church, I found that several unrealistic expectations were related to my time. The church was reluctant to let me use my agreed-on vacation time. Now, years later, I will get reprimanded if I have any vacation time left at the end of the year! Over the years, I've worked to establish clear boundaries and to develop a culture that understands and values having a healthy pastor. A demanding church will constantly pull a pastor away from his family, and if a church will not change the way it relates to you, this is a warning sign that problems lie ahead. You'll need to exercise discernment and have some honest conversations with church leaders to determine whether the expectations are coming from the church or if your own conscience is creating the demand.

When our oldest daughter was three years old, she contracted pneumonia, which required hospitalization. Wednesday evening came around, and I had to choose whether to teach Bible study that evening or return to the hospital to help my wife care for our sick daughter. I was still fairly new at our church, but I knew the church well enough to know they would have gladly excused my absence that evening so I could be with my family. Yet I chose to be at church instead. I even ignored the counsel of my associate pastor, who offered to teach in my place that night. The only pressure to be at church that evening was my own misguided conscience, not the church's expectation. Yes, churches can be demanding. But make sure you separate your own expectations from the expectations of your church. You may be surprised to learn that many of the demands you live with (and complain about) are actually your own self-inflicted ones.

4. You find yourself with a regretful heart. I confess that I love spending time with older pastors. I seek counsel from them, ask them for advice, and learn from their stories. When I talk to seasoned pastors who have grown kids, I often hear a common regret: "I wish I would have spent more time with my kids." Again, I know this can sound cliché after a while, but it's chilling to consider how common it is for pastors I admire and respect to say these words. Many of them would add that they felt this regret even while their kids were younger, but they ignored it because they were caught up in the rigors of ministry. Take some time to speak with older pastors. Learn from those who faithfully shepherded their children, as well as from those who have regretful, broken hearts. Hearing their pain can be a great gift to you. It can impress on you the consequences of your sin and encourage you to repent and change. It can cause you to empathize with those who are hurting. It may be the extra nudge you need to make a hard decision for the sake of your family.

As you read this, you may conclude it is too late for you. Your children are grown, your relationships are broken, and regret is all you have left. Remember that the gospel has the power to restore relationships. It restores us to our heavenly Father and has the power to restore any broken relationship in our lives — including any relationships with our children that have been harmed by the pressures of ministry. Even the most regretful pastor can channel his sorrow into prayer and hope that God can heal these damaged relationships, but it all begins with the grace of God in Christ. You need to receive the hope of the gospel as a humble, broken man.

Five Ways to Prevent Neglect

Warning signs help us assess the condition of our families and the quality of our care for them. They can also act as a motivator to be faithful. Yet the best remedy to combat family neglect is not just noticing a warning sign; it is taking action to reverse the pattern.

The hope of the gospel includes forgiveness and the newness of God's mercy every morning. Regardless of where you are right now, you can, by God's help, repent, change the patterns in your life, and put guards in place to prevent future neglect.

The good news of Jesus gives us hope that we really can change — that God can transform us and make us into new people. Here are five practical ways you can reverse the patterns in your life and prevent further neglect of your family. Doing these five things won't solve everything, but together with the power of the gospel and faith in Christ they can help you establish new patterns.

1. Take a day off every week. I start with this habit for several reasons. First, Sunday is a workday for every pastor. I know it is the Lord's Day. I know that some pastors are preaching on Sunday, and some are not. Regardless, while most of the people in your church are getting a break from their weekly grind on Sunday, the pastor is having one of his busiest days. Sunday is often a joyful day, but it can also be an emotionally draining day. It is far from low-key and restful.

Second, a pastor never really leaves his work behind. Regardless of how you spend your evenings or how hard you try to disconnect from the church, you never completely check out. The phone may not ring and no one may be stopping by, but the next sermon is still on your mind and heart; that elderly saint's battle with cancer still weighs on your shoulders; and when you leave the office, the burden of caring for others does not magically disappear until nine o'clock the next morning. The burdens may never completely leave, but having a day each week to focus primarily on your family is invaluable for long-term ministry stamina.

A final reason you need a day off every week, completely removed from your involvement in the church, is because it communicates that your family comes first — that they are a priority for you. A pastor's family makes many sacrifices. Having a day when your family knows they will have your undivided attention will communicate your love in ways that words never will. You show love for your wife and children by regularly scheduling a day to be with them, and then adhering to that commitment, regardless of how crazy things may be at the church.

{cara}

Make sure this day off is not just for family time but is also a day for your husband to rest from his weekly labors. It can be used for a date time with each other, fun family activities, and relaxing together at home. At times, we fall into the trap of trying to accomplish many tasks because it is Daddy's day off and we have his help. Even though your husband may be willing to do this, encourage him to truly take a day off. If some things on our to-do list have to wait, well, then those things have to wait. In the end, we won't remember the pile of laundry that didn't get done, but we will remember the time we missed out on with our husbands and our families.

·|·|· ·|·|· ·|·|·

2. Use all your vacation time. A couple of years ago, I was lovingly confronted by a dear friend and fellow pastor. He rebuked me for failing to use all of my vacation time. He gave me several reasons for taking every day of vacation the church gives me — something I had never done before.

He began by pointing out that vacation time is time set aside for me. Pastors never get a true break. They are constantly on call. Vacation time allows us to catch our breath, to get away from the madness and be refreshed. It's a time to rest. If you are a pastor, you likely know how useful you are when you are exhausted, distracted, and spent mentally and emotionally. Your vacation provides time for you to recharge. Use it wisely to achieve that end.

Vacation time also reaps benefits for your family. Just as important as a day set aside each week for personal rest are *extended* blocks of time when your family does not have to share you with the church. When you fail to use all of your church-approved vacation time, you rob your family from receiving from you an extended, focused time of care.

Vacation time is also for your church. Many pastors struggle with a complex that the church cannot survive without them. Using all your vacation time forces others to step up, shows them they can make it without you for a time, and reminds you that God is not dependent on you for the church to function. Pastors are expendable, and we need regular doses of humility to remind us of our expendability.

3. Enjoy every minute. As I drank coffee with a dear pastor friend of mine, I began to update him on my family. I shared how we were moving out of the baby/toddler stage with our four children and were enjoying a new season of life with several fun activities, watching our kids become "little people." As I shared this update, I noticed that my friend had tears in his eyes. He said, "I wish I would have enjoyed my kids more when they were little." This was a man I knew — a pastor who had done so much so well. He made time for his family. He spent individual time with each of his children. He showed up at their ball games and important events. By all outside appearances he could have been given the "Dad of the Year" award. Despite all of this, he confessed how much he had allowed the stress of ministry to distract his mind while he was with his children, particularly when they were young. They probably didn't even realize what had happened, but he did. And his children are now grown-ups who no longer live at home. "Those days of being with them every day," he said, "are gone."

I saw the sorrow in the face of this man — an amazingly faithful, well-known, and successful pastor. And as I recall his sorrow, it prompts me to do a serious "mind and heart check." Every time I leave church to go home to my family I am aware of the gift they are to me, and I try to enjoy every minute I can with them, in each stage of life.

There are many good and wonderful things you can do in your vocation. There are many blessings to pastoral ministry. I also know there is much to distract us. I know the good, godly burdens we are to carry are not magically removed when we go home. I also know many young pastors who are working overtime to try to prove to the skeptics that they are good and faithful. Still, at the end of the day, if we prove ourselves to others, we may have to pay a price we will later regret. Be faithful to your calling, but remember to enjoy your family. Treasure and value the precious stages in their life, for these are times that do not last long.

{cara}

Enjoy your husbands! When was the last time you sat back and thought about all the things you appreciate about your husband? When was the last time you thought about the pressures and demands he faces on a daily basis? When was the last time you thanked him for all he does for the family? When was the last time you went out and just enjoyed being with him? Our husbands need to know we not only desire to have them around but enjoy having them there. We need to resist the temptation to meet him at the door with our to-do list or our list of complaints about our day. Not that we can't share those things with him. We do need to think about what is the first thing we want our husband to experience when he walks in the door, and then we need to be deliberate to make that happen. What would you *expect when you came home after being gone all day? Make it a priority that his first five minutes home are pleasant ones.*

4. Just let the phone ring. I know this may sound simplistic, but there is great power in an unanswered phone call. I began a habit during our dinnertime of not answering calls. At first, I was unaware of the impact my tending to every phone call was having on my family. In the past, I always left the table to answer the phone, and when I left, they noticed. When I began to reverse my practice and chose not to answer it, they noticed that too. After a while, they asked me why I wasn't answering the phone. I said, "Because this is my time with you guys, and whoever it is can wait." When I saw the delightful and surprised looks on their faces, I realized the power of what I was doing. I was communicating that my time with them was valuable and important — more important than anything else. I even found that it was easier for them to give me up at other times because I had communicated their importance in a concrete way like this. I found I felt less guilty when I had to leave because I knew I had established this boundary. Try it yourself. When you make such an intentional, visible decision, you communicate in ways that words can't.

5. Evaluate the balance in your life. I know of no magic formula that will tell you when to work and when to give more time to your family. Regular conversations with your wife and kids are essential to find just the right balance between the distinctive needs of your family and your specific church or ministry context. The first and most insightful conversation will be with your wife. She knows how much you work and the needs of your family better than anyone. The next conversation could be with your fellow pastors or other acknowledged leaders in your church whom you trust. I provide updates to my fellow pastors both for my work and for the care of my family. These discussions give me accountability so that I work no more than sixty hours a week, take a day off every week, have family worship two to three times a week after dinner, and meet individually with each of my children on separate nights every week. Seek to find the balance that is right for you, your family, and your ministry. You may have to deliberately implement this plan with some discipline, and I would recommend having it assessed by those you trust.

{cara}

Wives, we need to be willing to speak up in these conversations. Seriously, you have to find your voice. Our husbands are not home all day long; therefore, we cannot expect them magically to know how the family is doing or what the family needs. We have to be willing to say, "This is just too much for us to handle." What are some of the warning signs that life is too busy? Well, usually it starts with our children misbehaving in unusual and extreme ways. Our children are children who misbehave at times, but they occasionally act out because of the stress in our life. They feel that stress too. Another way is when I start to feel overwhelmed and run-down. I try to push myself, but sometimes I just cannot keep going. I am convinced that God has designed me in this way to balance my husband and to give him a warning sign that he has pushed our family a bit too far with demands. However, he would never know these things if I didn't speak up and tell him. Now, I'm not suggesting you nag or yell at your husband, but that with humility you acknowledge you are not handling life very well. These are not easy conversations, but they are necessary conversations and very fruitful conversations.

The legacy a pastor leaves behind is ultimately not in his hands alone. We belong to a sovereign God who alone has the power to awaken the soul to the glory of Christ. Ultimately, God is the one who writes the story of our families. Billy Graham, though he has several regrets, would be the first to acknowledge God's grace at work in the lives of his children, despite his sin and failure as a father and husband. But the fact that God is sovereign and gracious should not motivate us to lose sight of our contribution. If anything, we should be even more motivated in light of God's mercy, moving from the amazing grace of the cross to loving sacrifice and faithful commitment to our wives and our children. You may have made mistakes, and you may be guilty of sinful neglect of your family, but there is still hope in the transforming power of the gospel. Turn to that hope today, knowing that the God who called you to be a pastor, a husband, and a father is faithful. He will save those who call out to him, and he is faithful to bless those who humbly seek him and rely on his grace.

Discussion Questions

For a Pastor and His Wife to Discuss Together

1. Which warning signs of neglect do we see in our lives?
2. Where do we struggle in our marriage? In what ways do we enjoy each other?
3. Where do we see evidence that our children love the church? Where are there signs that they resent it?
4. How balanced do we feel our family life is with our church life? What needs to change?
5. Which of the five practical applications to guard us from neglect are most important to implement?

Reflection

Thoughts from a PK

"Pastor's Kid"

How do you hold together the demands and tensions of life in the home of a faithful shepherd of Christ's sheep? My father contended for Christ outside and inside his home, caring for his wife and wrestling for the souls of his children even as he sought to care for God's flock and reach the lost. The pastor's calling makes his home a place in which the lowest points of sin and the highest points of grace seem to be placed in the closest company.

So I remember the scorn hurled by someone who criticized my father and his labors, and the tears of another who learned that we had thrown away the chair in which he had been sitting when converted. I remember those who seemed to presume that they were my father's only priority, and the tenderness and care with which my parents ministered to those who felt they were beyond help. I remember the sudden, urgent pastoral demands that could bring disappointment to children, and I remember my father on his knees in his study, pleading for us and others. I remember the apparent carelessness of some about attending the worship services, and my father's diligent preparation to preach Sunday by Sunday, morning and evening, week after week. I remember the viciousness of the charges sometimes laid at a faithful pastor's door, and the grief of that pastor as he mourned over the soul of the mudslinger.

A pastor's child often sees the worst of the world and the worst of the church. They see the thoughtlessness and carelessness of Christ's disciples in their weakness and sin. You cannot gild the Christian life when you live in a pastor's home, and my parents were too honest to try.

So as I grew up, and before I was converted to Christ, the world seemed painted in very dark colors. I accept the fact that not all pastors' children will share this experience, but I struggled not only with my own sin but with the sinfulness of others. It was only when a merciful God began to deal with my own heart that this began to change. Then I saw not only the ugliness of human sin but also the beauty of divine, sovereign grace—grace that was prominent in the lives of my parents and the ministry of my father.

After I was converted, I had no particular appetite to be a pastor, not least because I knew what was involved! But I also knew that our heavenly Father knows how to care for and vindicate his servants. I knew that my father's God was worth loving and serving—loving much and serving well. I knew the cost, but I also knew the joys, blessings, and rewards. If the pastor's child sees the worst, sometimes he also sees the best.

When I think of my father, I think of the description given of Nathanael: "An Israelite in whom there is no guile." My father is not a perfect man or a perfect pastor, and I stand a long way behind him. But the God we serve is altogether holy and utterly gracious, and his Son's grace is sufficient for his servants and their families. My father was far from sinless, but he always sought to serve Christ transparently and faithfully, and that is what pastors' children need to see. The best way to teach your children to love the church and its ministry is to love Jesus Christ, the Head of the church; to love the church, which is the body of Christ; and, to love with a Christlike love the family that the Lord has given to you. Ultimately, the stability and security of a pastor's child are found in a home and a family in which the father says, "As for me and my household, we will serve the LORD" (Joshua 24:15). Only when Christ is on his throne can everything else be well-ordered.

A pastor cannot entirely insulate his family from the realities of life in a sinful world, and I do not think he should try. Protection is his duty, but not deception. What he can and must do is point his children to Christ by his teaching and example and prayerfully train his children to live to the glory of God as they make their way through the world. And because the realities of sin and grace can be so prominent in a pastor's home, it provides a good platform from which to explain and to adorn the doctrine of God.

This reflection is written by a pastor's kid, who later grew up to become a pastor himself.

conclusion

faithful to family, fruitful in ministry

{brian}

Throughout this book, I have tried to challenge the common assumption that greatness in the kingdom of God is based on the perceived success or popularity of one's ministry. Instead, I have argued that success also depends on a man's faithfulness to serve humbly in the less glamorous areas of his life and calling. One of these less glamorous areas is the way a pastor cares for his family — loving and shepherding his wife and children.

Some may be tempted to believe it is impossible to have both outward success in ministry and a faithful ministry to their families, so as I conclude I highlight several men who are deemed great in the eyes of history and who also demonstrated great faithfulness in caring for their families. We would do well to imitate men like this, who both carried out fruitful ministries and tenderly cared for their families.

Though we do not have extensive records of their day-to-day life together, the written words of several pastors give evidence of a deep affection for their wives. For example, the eighteenth-century Baptist pastor Samuel Pearce made a significant effort to cherish his wife throughout the years of their marriage. He once wrote to her these words: "Every day improves not only my tenderness but my esteem for you. Called as I now am to mingle much with society in all its orders I have daily opportunity of making remarks on human temper and after all I have seen and thought my judgment as well as my affection still approves for you as the best of women for me ... I begin to count the days which I hope will bring me to a re-enjoyment of your dear company."[1]

We also find this pattern of cherishing and esteeming one's wife in the life of the great preacher and Southern Baptist Theological Seminary president, John Broadus. Broadus wrote openly and affectionately to his wife, Lottie, as if it would be his final words to her: "I'll tell you right now, here in the still night, in the room where at this hour we have often fallen asleep together, in the house where I first won your timid consent to be my bride, that I love you more now than ever before, more and more every year of the five — that I love you as much as I ever loved any other, or ever could have learned to love anyone that lives."[2]

Other pastors were such faithful examples to their families, leading them in worship and discipling them in their relationship with God. We see this in the commitment of Martyn Lloyd-Jones, one of the most influential preachers of the twentieth century, and in his regular pattern of prayer with his wife and children. Lloyd-Jones's biographer, Iain Murray, wrote, "Family prayer marked the close of every day, and after his death Bethan Lloyd-Jones was to say that it was here that she experienced her greatest loss."[3]

Probably one of the most powerful and influential examples of family care for me is seen in Richard Baxter, the great seventeenth-century English Puritan pastor. Baxter developed an unprecedented ministry reputation in Kidderminster by the way he tenaciously cared for the individual souls of his congregation. Although many know and have been influenced by Baxter's pastoral writings about caring for souls in the church (*The Reformed Pastor* is his classic work on the subject), few know about his amazing love for and commitment to his wife. They were married for nineteen years before she died unexpectedly at the age of forty-five. Coping with this great loss in his life, Baxter wrote a lover's tribute to his wife, Margaret. J. I. Packer, commenting on Baxter's tribute to his wife, had this to say: "[This] 'is undoubtedly the finest of Baxter's biographical pieces' [quoting one of Baxter's biographers], and one hopes that writing it benefited him as much as reading it can benefit us."[4]

Church history is filled with many men who were movers and shakers for the kingdom of God. They had great fruitfulness in their ministries and were quiet, faithful servants in their homes. The balance between both family and ministry they sought to capture by God's grace should remind each of us who pastor in the twenty-first century that this balance is possible — and it is worth pursuing at any cost. The transforming power of the gospel and of our biblically empowered calling before God is enough to aid all undershepherds of the Lord Jesus Christ to be faithful, not just to our ministries outside our homes, but within as well.

I leave you with this essential reminder: Your wife is the greatest earthly gift and asset that God has given you in both your ministry and your family life. She is the one who will lift you up when you are downcast. She will say the hard things to you that no one else will, challenge you when you are deceived, and remind the children of the value of your work when you are not home. And she will be there when others abandon you. Richard Baxter reminds us of the precious gift of a wife, writing as a pastor and widower of his love for his own wife:

> She was very desirous that we should all have lived in a constancy of devotion and a blameless innocency. And in this respect she was the meetest helper that I could have had in the world ... for I was apt to be over-careless in my speech and too backward to my duty, and she was always endeavoring to bring me to greater wariness and strictness in both. If I spoke rashly or sharply, it offended her; if I behaved (as I was apt) with too much neglect of ceremony, or humble compliment to any, she would modestly tell me of it; if my very looks seemed not pleasant, she would have me amend them (which my weak pained state of body undisposed me to do); if I forgot any week to catechize my servants and familiarly instruct them personally (besides my ordinary family duties [i.e., household prayers twice daily]), she was troubled at my remissness.[5]

As you set out to accomplish great things for the kingdom of God and to be faithful to your family, do not neglect to bring your wife, lover, and life companion along with you for the journey. She is God's greatest extension of grace in your daily life. Remind her and yourself of this truth regularly. And enjoy your life, your family, and your ministry together for the glory of God.

afterword

confessions of a pastor's wife

{cara}

When Brian and I were dating, I knew he wanted to be in ministry. In fact, at the time, he was an intern in a youth ministry. I remember specifically asking him if he desired to serve as a senior pastor, and he forcefully said, "No."

Yet here we are — he is now a senior pastor, and I am a pastor's wife.

I would have never chosen this life for myself. I had great fear and anxiety over the thought of assuming this role. I felt I could handle Brian serving in an associate position because I knew my family and I would not face the same expectations we would if he were the senior leader of a church.

You can imagine my surprise when Brian told me about a church looking for a senior pastor — and that he wanted to apply for the position. I thought to myself, *Really? Are you sure? Did I hear you right? Am I having a nightmare?*

I agreed to support his decision to apply, but I immediately began praying fervently that God would close that door. Instead, God pushed it open even wider. My anxiety quickly grew. It looked more and more like the pastor search committee was seriously considering Brian. He interviewed and preached, and before I knew it, he was offered the job. Within a matter of months, we had been interviewed, accepted the job, sold our house (which we had just built and only lived in for seven months), and moved to become involved in this new church.

Many things changed in me during this time. The more time I spent praying, asking God not to call my husband to this position, the more God worked on my own heart. Brian was clearly gifted to teach and preach, and he had a great desire to shepherd and care for people. I also knew he had a great desire to care for our family and me.

My biggest hesitation was my own fear. There were a lot of unknowns. How long could the church afford to pay us? Would any young families or young couples join our church when we were the only young family there? Who would help us with the work since we could not do it all on our own? But the biggest question I wrestled with was this: *How in the world will I handle being the wife of a pastor?* I doubted my own ability. I feared I wasn't up to the call.

I didn't feel equipped for the task before me. I had two young children, and I was pregnant with our third. I feared that our children would grow up resenting the life of a pastor's family, and I did not want them to be bitter about the church. I didn't know if I could handle people criticizing my husband. I didn't know if I could keep my mouth shut. I thought I would have to become a different person to fulfill this new role.

About a month before Brian was called to our church, I attended a conference. During that weekend, I spent much time in prayer. God was very gracious in giving me a peace about it all. He gently reminded me that not only was he in charge of where we were going and what we were doing, but he had already equipped me for this role. Though it didn't feel like it, God was already doing a work in me to equip me to be the wife my husband needed.

What I didn't realize in that moment was that I was only focusing on the hard and difficult things about life in ministry. We had been through some painful church situations already, and I was scared about the future, wondering if we would relive some of that pain. I didn't think I could handle it. I had my eyes turned so far inward that I had forgotten all the blessings that come with the role of being a pastor's wife.

Now that I have been in this role for several years, I find that my perspective has changed. In fact, I see how I've been blessed by the work God has done both in and through me. It feels good to know that God has used me to minister to someone. It feels good to know that my note really did encourage someone. It is a blessing to see church members not only caring for each other but caring for me, my husband, and our children. It is a blessing to be able to watch the body of Christ function as God intended.

Ministry is not easy. God has also used this experience to prune me and mature me — often painfully. At certain moments, I was not sure the doors of our church would remain open as we struggled in those first few years. At times, I felt like Brian and I were alone. Yet

God has graciously provided for us and brought about peace and unity in our church after some painful pruning.

I am thankful to be in this role because I have watched God work in some amazing ways that I would have completely missed otherwise. So though we do not know the future, we can always trust in God's good and wise plan for us, for our husbands, for our families, and for our churches. To God be the glory!

appendix 1

my battle with depression

{cara}

"So how long have you suffered with depression?"

I wish I could answer that question. The truth is that I am not sure. At times it seems like a lifetime. As a child I was always told that I was melancholy, and that description is true. I was a very quiet child. I tended to sit, listen, and observe others; I still do that. However, I tend to slip at times into a different kind of darkness.

My first major bout with depression came during my freshman year in college. My parents were divorced when I was three years old. I was feeling some pressure in my relationship with my dad, and I wasn't sure how to handle it. I became discouraged when I realized I could not make both my mom and my dad happy, no matter what decision I made. So I sought help through counseling. I don't remember the specifics of that time my counselor and I spent together, but I do know that God used it to bring me to a deeper level of brokenness and a greater realization of my dependence on him. As I look back on my time in college, I can clearly see times when God met me in very real ways.

Then I got married. My sweet husband knew I struggled with discouragement and felt down sometimes, but I usually rebounded quickly. We had been at our church for three years when I hit my next major bout with depression. My youngest child was born a month early, and we went through a year with various health issues with our children, resulting in several different surgeries and hospital stays. Drained to the point of exhaustion, I tried to care for four children, my husband, and our church; homeschool our kids; and go to a bazillion doctors' appointments. I was overwhelmed with my life and felt like I was failing in everything I did.

No matter what I did or how I changed my schedule, I just could not do it all. After a year of struggling (yes, it took me a whole year to finally admit I needed help), I came to a place where I had to share with my husband what was going on. I was depressed — not just down, but depressed. I was in a place of darkness where there seemed to be no hope, happiness, or joy.

Back to counseling I went — only this time, my husband came too. He had noticed my struggle but wasn't sure how to help me deal with it. Counseling was helpful. I saw how much I try to earn God's favor. I struggle with perfectionism and am frustrated with myself when I am anything less than perfect. I tend to dismiss the encouraging comments from my husband and from other church members and tend to replace them with self-loathing thoughts, such as *If they only knew the thoughts I have, or if they only knew what kind of person I really am, then they wouldn't say those things.* I was choosing to believe lies instead of believing God's truth about who I am in him and about how he sees me as his beloved child.

After several months of counseling, the darkness lifted. I experienced a joy I had missed for months. I experienced peace and a renewed love for God and his Word. I found a joy in serving our family and our church that had not been there for a long time. I found freedom in not having to please myself. But the battle did not end.

Please understand that I still had the thoughts creep into my head that I wasn't good enough or that I had failed again. However, I also had God's Word to remind me of the truth of my freedom in Christ.

However, depression is a battle that does not go away. Depression is not easily or quickly cured. Though it can go as quickly as it came, it can also reappear as quickly as it disappeared. And so, once again, I find myself in the embrace of depression. I find myself back down in the pit of darkness and despair.

Why am I at this place again? I am not sure. For over a year now, I have struggled, at times more intensely than others, but the darkness has never completely lifted.

I have learned many lessons from this struggle. First, depression comes and goes, even for Christians. God allows us to be in darkness for a season, but he is always faithful to bring us out of it. He is there in the darkness, whether I feel him or not. He will not abandon me here.

Second, I need others to help me in my struggle. I have a few very close friends who know intimately my struggle with depression. When I get to these places of depression, these dear Christian women know they need to check on me and remind me of God's truth. They often spend time speaking God's Word into my life and reminding me of his care for me. They spend time praying both with me and for me. They are invaluable helpers in my fight with depression.

Third, my husband loves me, despite my fight with depression. I am often tempted to worry that my husband will be disappointed to see me struggle. I am still in shock when he finds joy in caring for me through it all. I do recognize that my struggle is hard on him as well. His care for me does not come without great sacrifice on his part. He proactively seeks the help and counseling I need. He deliberately cares for me and encourages me, even when I don't receive his care and encouragement. He has not given up on me.

Fourth, my family doctor has been invaluable in helping me with my struggle. She often is one of the first to recognize the signs of my depression. She has worked with me to make sure there are no other underlying physical causes as a source of my depression. For example, blood test results showed I had a very low vitamin B-12 level, depression being a side effect of this condition. Raising my B-12 levels did not solve my depression issues completely, but treatment of this does play an important role in dealing with depression. She also encourages me to persevere. My doctor has often reminded me that it is not uncommon for pastors and their wives to struggle in these ways, for she has treated many of them. It is invaluable to have a like-minded medical person to help you with your struggles.

Fifth, and most important of all, I am constantly reminded of my complete and utter dependence on God. He is the one who has to sustain me in these times. He is the only one who can bring me up from the pit. I cannot do this Christian life on my own apart from God. One of my friends pointed out that depression is actually a gift from God because it leaves us in a place of humility and brokenness that cannot be achieved in other ways. It is in these places that God begins deep healing of old wounds. Without depression, I would never take the time to allow God into those hurtful places. I know that God will not leave me here forever, though if he chooses to, I also know he will sustain me through it each day. God is good and faithful, even in these trying times.

My struggle with depression is not the result of being a pastor's wife. If my husband had another vocation, I believe I would still struggle. However, being a pastor's wife (as well as being a pastor) intensifies this struggle. The exhausting nature of caring for the church, the temptation to carry the burdens of those who are struggling, the demands on our time and on our family, and the spiritual battle we face daily all contribute to exhaustion and vulnerability. This exhaustion is intensified as we try to do all these things in our own strength, apart from God. Therefore, to see pastors and their wives struggling with depression is not uncommon.

So let me encourage you if you find yourself in this place. First of all, you are not alone. Many Christians have very real struggles with depression and have over the whole course of human history. You can be a Christian — even a strong, mature Christian — and be depressed.

Next, let me encourage you to get help with your battle, which cannot be won by yourself. This battle demands encouragement, counseling, and prayer — and sometimes medical treatment. You have to be courageous enough to speak up and admit your struggle. You can't get help unless you ask for help. However, the irony of depression is that sometimes we are unable to ask for help. So if you know someone who is depressed, reach out and offer help.

Depressed people shouldn't be forgotten. Even though they may be silent, they are suffering—and many times they suffer alone. If you are struggling, find a friend in whom to confide. Talk with your spouse about it and start sharing your struggle instead of staying silent. We have to be honest about our struggle, but we need others to ask us about it as well.

Finally, let me encourage you that God knows your need. He knows where you are, and he will be faithful to you in these moments. The work Christ did on the cross provides forgiveness for our sins and shortcomings and gives us the freedom to walk with God and not lose his favor. The work Christ did provides healing for our souls. You are not alone in your struggle. You are not alone in your darkness. You are not alone in your pain. God is real, and his people do care. And he will bring you through this struggle with a greater love and dependence on him.

appendix 2

before becoming a pastor

{brian}

Aspiring pastors are usually chomping at the bit to become pastors — rightly so. Because of this eagerness, those aspiring to pastoral ministry often dream of one day serving in that capacity and miss significant ways they can serve their wives right now — ways they won't be able to serve once they become pastors dedicated to weekly preaching assignments.

Here are a few of those ways:

1. Sit with your wife in church every chance you get. If you asked a pastor's wife what her greatest desire is while on vacation, she might say, "I want to sit with my husband during church." This desire is why *a pastor should not preach while on vacation.* If you are not regularly preaching on Sundays, do all you can to sit with your wife. A day will come when you can't. You and your wife will be glad for that season in your life when you made that a priority.

2. Stay home on Sunday with sick kids. This act of service is a wonderful way for any man to serve his wife when the kids are little. In fact, one of our pastors modeled this well throughout his time at our church. He sent his wife to church, while he stayed home with their sick kids so she could go to hear the gospel proclaimed. My wife always stays home on Sundays when our kids are sick. I am preaching, so I have to be there. Until that day comes, serve your wife in these moments. She will be grateful.

3. Serve as the kids' caregiver during the service. One of my wife's most overlooked roles in church is to care for our children by herself during the service. Most husbands and wives work together to deal with children who sit with them, but not my wife. She does it on her own so I can preach. When you sit with your wife during the service, take initiative to correct any behavior problems and answer any irrelevant questions your children may ask in the middle of the sermon. Be the one to escort them out of the service if necessary. A day is coming when your wife will be flying solo on these things.

Aspiring pastors, I am glad you are eager to dive into pastoral ministry. You should be. Serving God's people in the weekly public ministry of the Word is a joy. However, do not allow your ambition for this work to cause you to miss some simple but practical ways to love and care for your wife now.

acknowledgments

Brian and Cara would like to thank . . .

- all who kindly served us by reading through this manuscript and giving valuable feedback throughout its various stages — a special thanks to Jason Adkins, who read this manuscript early on, thus doing much of the heavy lifting.
- the Anyabwiles, as well as those who contributed a Reflection — thank you for your friendship, partnership, and valuable contribution to this book.
- Zondervan, for being willing to partner with us on this book — we are thankful for the opportunity to work with you.
- the many pastors and their wives who patiently gave us time to seek their counsel and benefit from their wisdom — much of this book has your imprint, and we are grateful for your friendship and investment in us.
- our congregation, Auburndale Baptist Church, whom we have served for the last decade — we count it a great joy to know you and share our lives with you. Thank you for your gracious spirit toward us as we have stumbled around learning how to love and care for you. Thank you for your support and encouragement, not just to us, but to our children as well.

- our families — you have consistently supported us and the ministry to which we have been called by God. We thank you for encouraging us through many tears and trials and for rejoicing with us through the joys of answered prayer. Thank you for praying for us and with us. We especially thank our children, who gladly and selflessly gave up both Mom and Dad so we could work on this project. Thank you for your patience as we learn how to be better parents to you and for your forgiveness when we have failed. We are thankful for the work God is doing in each of you. We treasure you as our blessings from God.
- the one true living God and our Savior and Redeemer, Jesus Christ. May you use this book to strengthen the marriages and families of your shepherds until you, the Chief Shepherd, return for your bride.

notes

Front Matter

1. Samuel D. Proctor and Gardner C. Taylor, *We Have This Ministry: The Heart of the Pastor's Vocation* (Valley Forge, Pa.: Judson, 1996), 49 – 50.

2. Doreen Moore, *Good Christians Good Husbands? Leaving a Legacy in Marriage and Ministry* (Ross-shire, Scotland: Christian Focus, 2004), 32.

3. Ibid., 33.

4. This statement comes only from personal observations, having spent my entire upbringing in Methodist churches and learning the Methodist system of appointing pastors.

5. Arnold Dallimore, *George Whitefield: The Life and Times of the Great Evangelist of the 18th Century Revival*, vol. 2 (Carlisle, Pa.: Banner of Truth, 2004), 110.

6. Ibid., 112.

7. Ibid., 113.

8. Moore, *Good Christians Good Husbands?* 10.

Chapter 1: The Problem

1. Dr. Richard J. Krejcir, "Statistics on Pastors: What Is Going On with the Pastors in America," www.intothyword.org/articles_view.asp?articleid=36562&columnid= (accessed January 15, 2013).

2. Paul David Tripp, *Dangerous Calling: Confronting the Unique Challenges of Pastoral Ministry* (Wheaton, Ill.: Crossway, 2012), 22.

3. Pragmatism is a method of doing ministry that focuses on doing what seems to work, often at the expense of what is biblically faithful.

4. Cited in Krejcir, "Statistics on Pastors."

5. This biblical teaching on the effects of sin on the heart (Mark 7) was first published in my booklet, "Help, He's Struggling with Pornography" (Day One Publishing). It needs to be acknowledged that the wording is very similar here but is focused more specifically on the heart of pastors in this context.

Chapter 2: The Solution

1. The gospel is the good news of Jesus Christ in which his perfect life, atoning death on the cross, and victorious resurrection have satisfied the wrath of God on sin. Therefore, anyone who repents and believes in Jesus Christ through faith alone in his person and work is forgiven from all sin, clothed in Christ's righteousness, and eternally adopted as a child of God.

2. Charles Ray, *Mrs. C. H. Spurgeon* (Pasadena, Tex.: Pilgrim, 2003), 53.

3. Ibid.

4. Ibid.

Chapter 3: The Struggle

1. My favorite is Carolyn Mahaney's *Feminine Appeal: Seven Virtues of a Godly Wife and Mother*, rev. ed. (Wheaton, Ill.: Crossway, 2012).

Chapter 4: Caring for Your Wife

1. David B. Calhoun, *Princeton Seminary: The Majestic Testimony 1869 – 1929* (Carlisle, Pa.: Banner of Truth, 1996), 2:315 – 16

2. Ibid., 316.

3. C. H. Spurgeon, Susannah Spurgeon, and W. J. Harrald, *C. H. Spurgeon's Autobiography*, vol. 3 (Pasadena, Tex.: Pilgrim, 1992), 183 – 84.

Chapter 6: Shepherding Together

1. Charles H. Spurgeon, *Autobiography, Volume 1: The Early Years, 1834–1859* (Edinburgh: Banner of Truth, 1962), 43 – 45; see www.spurgeon.org/earlyimp.htm (accessed January 18, 2013).

2. Douglas F. Kelly, "Family Worship: Biblical, Reformed, and Viable for Today," in *Worship in the Presence of God*, ed. Frank J. Smith and David C. Lachman (Greenville, S.C.: Greenville Seminary Press, 1992), 112.

3. Martin Luther, *Luther's Works, Volume 4: Lectures on Genesis: Chapters 21 – 25*, ed. Jaroslav Pelikan (Saint Louis, Mo.: Concordia, 1964), 384.

4. This is one reason we provide our church members with the passage

that will form the text for the upcoming Sunday's sermon. We want them to prepare themselves and their families for the church's next public gathering.

5. George Marsden, *Jonathan Edwards: A Life* (New Haven, Conn.: Yale University Press, 2004), 133, 321.

Chapter 7: Shepherding Looking Forward

1. Doreen Moore, *Good Christians Good Husbands? Leaving a Legacy in Marriage and Ministry* (Ross-shire, Scotland: Christian Focus, 2004), 136

2. Cited in "Biographies: William (Billy) F. Graham," Billy Graham Evangelistic Association, www.billygraham.org/biographies_show.asp?p=1&d=1 (accessed January 18, 2013).

3. Billy Graham, *Just As I Am: The Autobiography of Billy Graham* (New York: HarperCollins, 1997), 702–3.

4. Ibid., 710.

Conclusion

1. Michael A. G. Haykin, *The Christian Lover* (Lake Mary, Fla.: Reformation Trust, 2009), 66.

2. Ibid., 80.

3. Iain Murray, *D. Martyn Lloyd-Jones: The Fight of Faith: 1939–1981* (Edinburgh: Banner of Truth, 1990), 763.

4. J. I. Packer, *A Grief Sanctified: Through Sorrow to Eternal Hope* (Wheaton, Ill.: Crossway, 2002), 12.

5. Ibid., 37.

Share Your Thoughts

With the Author: Your comments will be forwarded to the author when you send them to *zauthor@zondervan.com*.

With Zondervan: Submit your review of this book by writing to *zreview@zondervan.com*.

Free Online Resources at

www.zondervan.com

Daily Bible Verses and Devotions: Enrich your life with daily Bible verses or devotions that help you start every morning focused on God. Visit www.zondervan.com/newsletters.

Free Email Publications: Sign up for newsletters on Christian living, academic resources, church ministry, fiction, children's resources, and more. Visit www.zondervan.com/newsletters.

Zondervan Bible Search: Find and compare Bible passages in a variety of translations at www.zondervanbiblesearch.com.

Other Benefits: Register to receive online benefits like coupons and special offers, or to participate in research.

ZONDERVAN®